4-20-07
Ages 9-12

THE "MISSISSIPPI BURNING" CIVIL RIGHTS MURDER CONSPIRACY TRIAL

A Headline Court Case

Headline Court Cases

THE "MISSISSIPPI BURNING" CIVIL RIGHTS MURDER CONSPIRACY TRIAL

A Headline Court Case

Harvey Fireside

MISSING **CALL FBI**

THE FBI IS SEEKING INFORMATION CONCERNING THE DISAPPEARANCE AT PHILADELPHIA, MISSISSIPPI, OF THESE THREE INDIVIDUALS ON JUNE 21, 1964. EXTENSIVE INVESTIGATION IS BEING CONDUCTED TO LOCATE GOODMAN, CHANEY, AND SCHWERNER, WHO ARE DESCRIBED AS FOLLOWS:

ANDREW GOODMAN   JAMES EARL CHANEY   MICHAEL HENRY SCHWERNER

Enslow Publishers, Inc.

40 Industrial Road	PO Box 38
Box 398	Aldershot
Berkeley Heights, NJ 07922	Hants GU12 6BP
USA	UK

http://www.enslow.com

For Ella Rose, Noah Isadore, Sophie Jane—
our hopes for the future.

Library of Congress Cataloging-in-Publication Data

Fireside, Harvey.
  The "Mississippi Burning" civil rights murder conspiracy trial : a headline court case /
Harvey Fireside.
    p. cm.—(Headline court cases)
Summary: Examines the trials of the men accused of murdering three civil rights work-
ers in Mississippi in 1964, including the Supreme Court decision to try defendants in a
federal rather than a state court and the final verdicts which marked the first time, in
Mississippi, that a jury convicted white men for killing African Americans or civil rights
workers.
Includes bibliographical references and index.
  ISBN 0-7660-1762-1
1. Trials (Murder)—Mississippi—Meridian—Juvenile literature. 2. Civil rights movements—Mississippi—History—Juvenile literature. [1. Trials (Murder) 2. Civil rights
movements—Mississippi—History. 3. African Americans—Civil rights—Mississippi.] I.
Title. II. Series.
  KF224.M47 F57 2002
  345.73'02523—dc21

                            2002000389

Printed in the United States of America

10 9 8 7 6 5 4

To Our Readers:
We have done our best to make sure that all Internet addresses in this book were active
and appropriate when we went to press. However, the author and publisher have no
control over and assume no liability for the material available on those Internet sites or on
other Web sites they may link to. Any comments or suggestions can be sent by e-mail to
comments@enslow.com or to the address on the back cover.

Illustration Credits: All photos are from Library of Congress, except for the
following: Charles Harrington, Cornell University Photography, p. 73; Harris
and Ewing, Collection of the Supreme Court of the United States, pp. 56, 61;
Lyndon Baines Johnson Library, p. 82; Mississippi Department of Archives
and History, p. 3; National Archives and Records Administration, pp. 24, 35, 67;
Bill Reed/Stockphoto.com, p. 62.

Cover Illustration: Mississippi Department of Archives and History.

Contents

chapter one

THREE MISSING CIVIL RIGHTS WORKERS

FREEDOM SUMMER— Three civil rights workers were heading to Longdale, a small farming community in Neshoba County, Mississippi, on June 21, 1964. James Chaney, a young African-American man who knew the back roads well, was driving the blue Ford station wagon. His two companions—Michael Schwerner (known as "Mickey") and Andrew Goodman (called "Andy")—were his white, Jewish coworkers in the Congress of Racial Equality (CORE), a group founded in 1942 to bring about social change by nonviolent means. That summer, hundreds of volunteers from northern college campuses were heading to Mississippi to help African Americans register to vote. Many state and local leaders had pledged to use intimidation and legal means to keep African-American citizens from ever voting or sending their children to integrated (mixed race) schools. They saw the "invasion" of students from the North as a threat to the established Southern way of life, where whites were in control.

Mickey Schwerner had volunteered the previous November with his wife, Rita, to help African Americans in the South gain the civil rights guaranteed by the U.S. Constitution. He had studied at Cornell University and at Columbia University's Graduate School of Social Work. Then he worked at an interracial housing project on the Lower East Side in New York City. He had put in many hours counseling children and going to court with those in legal trouble. He had also participated in demonstrations for civil rights. At one of these he had been arrested while picketing a building project for excluding African-American workers. Although he was sentenced to sixty days in jail, he had been released on appeal and the charges continued indefinitely. (In effect, the charges were dropped.)

Mickey and Rita Schwerner had decided to leave their jobs in New York after seeing pictures of demonstrators in Birmingham, Alabama, being attacked by police with dogs and fire hoses. Their final decision came after learning of the murder of four little girls in a Birmingham church that was firebombed on September 15, 1963.[1] The Schwerners were hired by CORE for a salary of $9.80 a week, plus food and lodging from local African-American families. Robert Moses, program director of the Council of Federated Organizations (COFO), had assigned them to Meridian, the second-largest city in Mississippi.

By this time—June 1964—Mickey and Rita Schwerner had been in Meridian for six months. Their honesty, friendliness, and hard work had earned them the respect of African Americans such as James Chaney in the six counties around Meridian. Chaney had dropped out of school and was working part time as a plasterer, like his dad, until he volunteered for civil rights work. Some of the people who had offered the Schwerners shelter, however, had been threatened by their white employers. So, Mickey and Rita had to move. At their last house, their water, gas, and electricity had been periodically cut off, a sign from the white people controlling the utility companies that they were definitely not welcome.

Their phone lines were often tied up by hate calls, evidently from members of the Ku Klux Klan (KKK), a secret organization violently opposed to racial integration.

Despite the anger and hostility they had encountered, the Schwerners could also look back on real accomplishments. They had set up a community center of five rooms, where African Americans had a private place to meet, read books, make clothes for themselves on a sewing machine, learn how to apply for a job, and learn how to register to vote. When Mickey and Rita Schwerner could not find another apartment to rent, they slept on cots at this center. Whenever funds ran low, they would get by with soda and bread, sometimes with cheese, as their supper.[2]

Volunteer Training

In early June 1964, the Schwerners and James Chaney had gone to the Western College for Women in Oxford, Ohio. The National Council of Churches had chosen that campus as the site to train volunteers for the Mississippi Freedom

Summer Project. They were planning to attend the training sessions and to recruit at least one newcomer to join them in Meridian. The most promising of the volunteers was Andrew Goodman, a twenty-year-old student at Queens College who had studied drama and politics. Mickey Schwerner thought that Andy Goodman would be just the right person to run a Freedom School in the African-American community of Longdale. At Freedom Schools, young people were taught reading and writing skills to help them get decent jobs and perhaps pass the tests for voter

In 1964, hundreds of students from college campuses in the North volunteered for the Mississippi Summer Freedom Project. Here, volunteers listen to team leader Charlie McLaurin talk about voter registration work.

registration. At first, Goodman was drawn to a different project, in a town where he would help set up a craft workshop. Then he came back with Mickey Schwerner and James Chaney. Rita Schwerner would stay behind at Oxford to help train the next group of volunteers.

Soon after they checked into the Meridian center, Mickey Schwerner, Andy Goodman, and James Chaney set off for Longdale. They wanted to check out a disturbing news report, that fire had burned down the church that was supposed to house the Freedom School. They followed the precautions that had been part of their training. The three men told the staff people in Meridian to call all the police stations and jails in the area if they were not back by 4:00 P.M. If such a search was unsuccessful, the staff would notify the federal authorities in Washington that something had gone wrong. There had been other incidents in which civil rights workers had been arrested under false pretenses, then beaten while being held in local jails. It was no secret that many Mississippi police officers and even state highway patrolmen were members of the KKK.

Church Burning

When they got to Longdale, the three found that the Mount Zion Church had, in fact, been burned to the ground. (It would be the first of twenty African-American churches to be firebombed that summer.) The FBI investigation of this series of arson and physical attacks was named Mississippi Burning, MIBURN for short. Thirty masked and hooded Klansmen armed with rifles and shotguns had set the fire only after making it clear that they wanted to find Mickey Schwerner, whom they called "Goatee" because of his small beard.[3] They were angry because they could not find any civil rights workers there. So, they dragged out ten African Americans attending a business meeting at the church—seven men and three women—and beat them. They had spared only one old woman who was kneeling while praying aloud. The four African-American members of the congregation who told Mickey Schwerner what happened said that members of the KKK were still looking for him.

Schwerner did not give up easily. The church could be rebuilt. Perhaps the Freedom School could be set up in the meantime in temporary quarters. But first, the three had to return to Meridian to check in and make new plans. Longdale was in Neshoba County, a poor rural area where civil rights workers were at greater risk than those in the city were. Both the sheriff, Lawrence Rainey, and his deputy, Cecil Price, were known to be members of the KKK.[4] Speakers at the Oxford training sessions had said that the student volunteers needed to be very careful. John Doar, deputy chief of the Justice Department's Civil Rights Division, praised the students who had "given their time and energy and dedication to correct the very bad and evil problems in the South," namely, "the way in which American Negro citizens are treated before the law." But they should not expect the federal government to protect them. The FBI, he said, was "an investigative agency and not a police force."[5]

R. Jess Brown, one of the four African-American attorneys who practiced in Mississippi, had warned the

Student volunteers stand outside a chapel that was fire-bombed in Ruleville, Mississippi, in 1964. The town's mayor said that African-American church members "did it themselves to get attention."

volunteers that they could expect hostility from the police in the state: "They'll arrest anybody." If students thought they could explain constitutional law to a local sheriff with a second-grade education, they were wrong. Whites could expect even rougher treatment than African Americans. "You're going to be classified into two groups in Mississippi: niggers and nigger-lovers. And they're tougher on nigger-lovers."[6]

James Forman, the executive secretary of the Student Nonviolent Coordinating Committee (SNCC), had been even more blunt about the summer campaign. He said, "I may be killed and you may be killed. If you recognize that, the question whether we're put in jail will become very, very minute."[7]

Robert Moses, a field secretary for the SNCC, had worked in Mississippi since 1961. He told the students the best they could hope for was to build public pressure on agencies of the federal government to become more directly involved. In the meantime, they should avoid arousing hostile reactions by making clear their work was voter registration, not organizing sit-ins or protest marches. Cordell Reagon, another African-American field secretary, said, "They take you to jail, strip you, lay you on the floor and beat you until you're almost dead. They'll beat you because you're white. They wouldn't do that to me."[8]

The "Cautious" Route

With these recent warnings in mind, the three men in the station wagon decided on a safer route back to Meridian than the highway on which they had come. Route 491 was the most direct way to travel the thirty-five miles back. But it was a clay road, with many intersecting dirt roads on which attackers could be waiting. So, at around 3:00 P.M., they turned off onto Highway 16, a blacktopped road that would take them through Philadelphia, the Neshoba County seat.

Unfortunately, Deputy Sheriff Price spotted their well-known station wagon heading west, just outside Philadelphia. He made a U-turn and pursued it. Just inside the city limits, he pulled the car over to the side of the road. What happened next depends on whose version of conflicting accounts is to be believed. Deputy Price said that he arrested the three men because they had been driving over the speed limit. Supposedly they were going 65 miles per hour in a 30-mile-per-hour zone.[9] This is unlikely, however. They had been trained to strictly observe all driving laws, in order to stay out of trouble. In addition, Price would have had no reason, in that case, to detain the two others. Only Chaney, the driver, would have been responsible for the violation.

Two Mississippi Highway Patrol officers gave a different version of the events. They said they had been radioed by Sheriff Price that he had arrested three suspects "for investigation." This sounds more likely, since it gave Price an opportunity to check with his confederates in the KKK. His prize catch was Mickey Schwerner, who had eluded the KKK in the raid on Mount Zion Church five days earlier. Chaney and Goodman were simply unfortunate enough to be caught together with Schwerner. What were they suspected of? In a bizarre explanation, Price was later quoted as saying that they were being investigated for burning down the Mount Zion Church.[10] It was not unusual for Southern authorities to claim that violence against civil rights workers had been self-inflicted in order to gain publicity. All sources agree that Price led the way to the Philadelphia jail in his patrol car. The two highway police officers followed, one of them with Chaney in the station wagon, the other with Schwerner and Goodman in his car. It has also been established that the three prisoners were booked into the county jail. Schwerner and Goodman were in a front cell with another white prisoner arrested for drunkenness. Chaney was in a back cell with another "disorderly" African

American prisoner. Price told Inspector King, the highway patrol superior of the two officers, that he was holding all three for seventy-two hours, the legal limit for an investigative arrest. That evening, the three civil rights workers did not seem to have cause for concern—yet. They had been given dinner, and they had every reason to hope that someone from their office would locate them with a prearranged phone search after 4:00 P.M. (It became known later that someone had called the jail asking about the three men. But whoever answered denied knowing anything about them.)

Last Moments Alive

It was only later at night that the situation changed. Around 10:15 P.M., the three prisoners were told they would be released if Chaney, the driver, would pay the twenty dollar fine for speeding. It was customary for county sheriffs to collect such fines. The money served as part of their salary. Chaney did not have that amount, so Schwerner was allowed to pass him the money. It appears, according to the official version of the events of that night, that they were free, although they might have been exposed to whatever dangers awaited them on the dark roads ahead. This version of events is also in question. If the three men had really walked out of the jail, they most likely would have gone to the public phone next to a nearby hotel on the town square, to report their situation to the other civil rights workers in their office. It is therefore possible that they were not really freed, but taken in handcuffs by Deputy Price to an unknown destination. In any case, we do know that Schwerner,

Chaney, and Goodman were never seen alive again, except by their killers.

News of the disappearances made headlines two days later, on June 23. Civil rights workers in Meridian had sounded the alarm on the night of June 21. The coordinator for the SNCC in Atlanta, Georgia, was a volunteer named Mary King. She had called every jail and detention center in the area of Mississippi where the three had last been seen.[11] No one, not even Deputy Price who had arrested them, admitted they knew anything about the three missing civil rights workers. The Mississippi State Highway Patrol had issued a missing persons bulletin but announced that they had no plans for further action. The U.S. Justice Department, which Mary King had also alerted, ordered a full-scale search by the FBI on June 22. A spokesperson said, "We are investigating the possibility that they are being held against their will by persons who are not law-enforcement officers or that they are otherwise being deprived of their civil liberties."[12] In other words, the worst was expected. However, the Neshoba County sheriff, Lawrence Rainey, sounded unconcerned: "If they're missing, they just hid somewhere, trying to get a lot of publicity out of it, I figure." His deputy, Cecil Price, said that he escorted them along Highway 19 en route to Meridian. "I told them to leave the county," he recounted.[13]

Meanwhile, Rita Schwerner flew back to Meridian from Oxford, Ohio. She and the parents of the three missing men appealed to the White House for help with the search. The FBI agents were joined by sailors searching the Bogue

The Freedom Summer volunteers were trained in methods of nonviolent resistance. Here, at a course in Oxford, Ohio, participants are taught to protect themselves by curling up in a fetal position during a beating.

Chitto Swamp near Philadelphia. They were also using helicopters from a nearby naval base. When John Lewis, national chairman of the SNCC, offered to add student volunteers to the search, he was officially discouraged. White citizens of Neshoba County were heard threatening the newsmen who had come to Philadelphia and telling them to leave the county.[14] These citizens told a reporter they did not think the disappearance of the three civil rights workers deserved all this attention.

Burned-Out Car Found

Then, on June 24, the story took a turn for the worse. The FBI found the 1964 Ford station wagon that the three men had been driving. It had been severely burned and left fifteen miles northeast of Philadelphia, in a swamp off Bogue Chitto Creek. The search for the men, or at least their bodies, continued. President Lyndon B. Johnson issued a statement: "All the forces of our society, both state and Federal, must be directed to preserving law and order. The President shares the anxiety and deep distress of the parents of these young men."[15] President Johnson met with the Schwerner and Goodman parents for twenty minutes at the White House. He told them he had ordered the FBI to spare no effort in locating the missing men. Yet he did not say what the parents of other student volunteers wanted to hear: that the federal government would take responsibility for protecting them. To do that, federal officials commented, would turn the clock back a hundred years to the days of Reconstruction, when federal troops occupied the South.[16]

To indicate his concern, President Johnson had also talked to Mississippi governor Paul B. Johnson. The governor had assured the president that the state's law enforcement personnel would prevent acts of violence. He also agreed to meet presidential representative Allen Dulles, former director of the Central Intelligence Agency (CIA), who was being sent from Washington D.C., on June 24. These official actions seemed designed to reassure the public that, despite protests by civil rights activists and their enemies in Mississippi, law and order would be maintained. But Governor Johnson had been elected in 1963 on a segregationist platform that clearly discriminated against African Americans. Federal officials were also aware that many state, county, and local police officers were members of the KKK. Any cooperation between these police forces and the FBI would, therefore, likely be extremely limited. In fact, there was a good chance that incriminating evidence would be made known to suspects or, even worse, that FBI informants would be silenced. Nor could Washington officials expect local judges and juries to convict those responsible for crimes against civil rights workers. They had never done so in this state.

By June 25, the search conducted by state troopers, sheriff's deputies, and the FBI for the missing men had not turned up any further clues. One federal agent told a newspaperman, "We're now looking for bodies."[17] The Johnson-Dulles meeting at the state capitol went well, as both gave statements of federal-state cooperation. However, the governor was trying to keep the federal presence in the state as limited as possible. The situation grew more tense when James Farmer, director of CORE, and John Lewis, chairman of SNCC, arrived in Neshoba County with thirty-three African Americans who volunteered to help in the search. A compromise was reached when Sheriff Rainey allowed only the leaders of the group to visit the ruins of Mount Zion Church and the burned station wagon. The volunteers were sent back to Meridian.

At the convention of the National Association for the Advancement of Colored People (NAACP) in Washington, Roy Wilkins, executive secretary, urged the Justice Department to offer protection to the 985,000 African Americans in Mississippi. Attorney General Robert F. Kennedy, however, said that the federal government could not take "preventive" police action. The best he could do was to increase the number of FBI agents in the state. This did not satisfy the eighteen hundred delegates who walked to the Justice Department.

Robert F. Kennedy, a brother of President John F. Kennedy, served as attorney general. He recommended that extremist groups such as the KKK should be closely watched as the volunteers for the Freedom Summer Project prepared to go south in June 1964.

Meanwhile, in New York, several hundred others marched to the U.S. Courthouse. Both groups asked for federal protection to stop lawlessness in Mississippi.

Civil Rights Precedent

President Johnson was not ready to send new federal forces into the state. Two former presidents had already reluctantly taken such action. President Eisenhower had used one thousand troops in September 1957 to escort nine African-American students to Central High School in Little Rock, Arkansas. He had also put the state's National Guard under his orders. Up to that point, Governor Orval Faubus had defied federal court orders to integrate the school. That had been the first time since Reconstruction that federal troops had been used to protect African-American citizens. President Kennedy, in September 1962, also was forced to overcome resistance to school integration. This time, Mississippi governor Ross Barnett adamantly refused to let James Meredith become the first African American ever to enroll at the University of Mississippi—"Ole Miss"— despite the order of a federal circuit court. It had taken two days for federal marshals, the state National Guard under federal command, and regular army troops to turn back the anti-Meredith mobs on the campus. During the struggle, two men were killed and at least 375 people were injured before the governor finally gave in.[18]

President Johnson was determined to enact a new civil rights bill, the strongest in nearly one hundred years. Partly to honor assassinated President Kennedy, the bill had received preliminary approval from the House of Representatives in February 1964. While Schwerner, Chaney, and Goodman were missing, the bill was still being fiercely debated in the House and the Senate. Federal intervention in Mississippi might defeat this bill that would expand protection of constitutional rights for African Americans. This may have been one factor in the slow pace of the FBI investigation into the missing men. Another factor, later recounted by John Doar, was that the citizens of Neshoba County would not tell the FBI what they knew. About half of the nearly one thousand people interviewed were known or suspected to be members of the KKK. They often sent agents off on wild goose chases, but mostly they kept quiet.[19]

Search Comes to a Close

After a month of fruitless efforts by one hundred agents, the FBI circulated an offer of a $30,000 reward (a huge amount of money at that time) and strict confidentiality to anyone who told it where the bodies were buried. The offer evidently brought results within a week. On August 4, forty-four days after it had begun, the search for the three missing men was coming to a close. A bulldozer appeared on a farm southwest of Philadelphia and began digging into an earthen dam. Near the center of this dam the ten-foot blade of the machine soon turned up a pair of men's boots in the clay. Not long after, the three partly decomposed bodies of Schwerner, Chaney, and Goodman were uncovered. Federal agents and local sheriffs helped to transport the remains to a coroner's lab to be examined. The three men had been

After more than a month, searchers found the remains of James Chaney, Andrew Goodman, and Michael Schwerner in an earthen dam on a farm in Philadelphia, Mississippi.

shot. Chaney's body also had broken bones, though it could not be determined conclusively if this was caused by a beating or by his burial.[20]

The anonymous source had led the agents to the burial site but he had not identified the murderers. It would take many more months before further reward offers by the FBI would bring out other informants. It would take even more time to build a case that could be presented in court. At least now, federal agents knew that the conspiracy of silence protecting the KKK in Mississippi could be breached. Neither conscience nor respect for law and order seemed to move people in Mississippi to fulfill their civic and moral responsibility to report evidence of criminal activity. But greed worked well.

chapter two

MISSISSIPPI—
CIVIL RIGHTS
BATTLEGROUND

PROTEST—James Lawson had been studying for the ministry at Vanderbilt University, a predominantly white school in Tennessee. Because Lawson took an active role in the African-American student movement in Nashville in 1960, he was expelled a few months before graduation. Several white faculty members at Vanderbilt resigned because of the school's refusal to readmit Lawson despite his strict practice of nonviolence. He had spent three years in India studying the nonviolent methods used by Mohandas K. ("Mahatma") Gandhi to win the country's independence. In June 1964, as a Methodist pastor in Memphis, Lawson told recruits preparing to take part in the Mississippi Freedom Summer Project, "Just your walking into Canton, Mississippi, or Ruleville or Shaw, just your being there, could be the catalytic agent that evokes violence."[1]

Why was this state so opposed to granting equal rights to its nearly one million African-American citizens?

Hodding Carter, a Pulitzer prize–winning editor from Greenville, Mississippi, offered one possible answer. He found that residents had for centuries believed "that whites are superior in every respect to Negroes." That accounted for the fact that "never in the state's history has a white man been found guilty of first-degree murder . . . when the slain person was black."[2] It seemed impossible to convict such killers when jury members were often linked by friendship and family ties to the defendant. Finally, there were community "pressures in a region which . . . demands a united white front against . . . invading students, the Federal judges

Police officers with dogs in Jackson, Mississippi, watch as a bus with young people protesting segregated bus travel arrives on May 25, 1961. These "freedom riders" were arrested and jailed as soon as they got off.

and agents, the alien ministers and the Negroes into whose heads these outsiders are putting such dangerous notions as their right to vote."[3]

The Ku Klux Klan

Much of the state and local justice system consisted of members of the White Knights of the Ku Klux Klan, a secret group sworn to oppose integration by threats or violence. The KKK was growing stronger in the 1960s. After three decades of inactivity, the Klan was rising up against civil rights victories being won by lawyers in the courts and protesters in the streets.

The KKK had originally appeared in the South in the aftermath of the Civil War to resist Union troops occupying the eleven Southern states. Soon it shifted from merely intimidating the newly freed slaves to inflicting punishments on those who tried to exercise their constitutional rights. Thousands of former slaves and their white allies were murdered.[4] As KKK groups attracted vigilante attackers and killers, they were formally disbanded in 1869 by their first leader, "Imperial Wizard" Nathan Bedford Forrest, a former Confederate general. But some of the local groups refused to obey his order. They gained power with the support of white plantation owners, who had lost the bloodiest war in the country's history. By the end of the Civil War, Mississippi had gone from being one of the wealthiest states to one of the poorest. The millions of dollars represented by its slaves as "property" had vanished.

In 1875, the white Democrats of Mississippi intimidated

enough African-American voters to regain control of the state government. President Ulysses S. Grant refused the governor's request for army assistance. The militia was not called in for fear of starting a race war.[5]

By 1877, the era of Reconstruction was definitely over. In order to win the disputed votes of Florida, South Carolina, and Louisiana in the 1876 presidential election, Rutherford B. Hayes offered to withdraw the remaining Union troops from the South. Without Northern troops to protect them, African Americans in these three states and in Mississippi, though in the majority of the population, quickly became a tiny minority of the electorate. State houses were again occupied by the old elite, enforcing the power of white citizens.[6]

Political and Economic Consequences of the Civil War

The consequences of the Civil War were both political and economic. The Fifteenth Amendment, adopted in 1870, had guaranteed that no state could deny citizens the vote "on account of race, color, or previous condition of servitude." But starting in the 1890s, Southern states made it virtually impossible for African Americans to register to vote, by requiring poll taxes and literacy tests. These tests asked applicants to interpret a complex clause of the state constitution. Mississippi held a state convention in 1890 designed to keep African Americans from voting. The new law required anyone trying to register to show his understanding of the state constitution by interpreting a clause of it to the satisfaction of the registrar. Overnight virtually all of the 123,000 African-American citizens in the state lost their right to vote.[7]

By the 1920s, Southern states also held "white primaries," which excluded African Americans. In most parts of the South, winning nomination by the Democratic party, with its solid majority, assured a candidate of being elected. Then there were gerrymanders, oddly drawn boundaries of electoral districts that submerged pockets of African American voters in a sea of white voters. Finally, until they were banned by the Twenty-fourth Amendment in 1964, poll taxes in Mississippi kept away most African Americans (as well as poor whites), who could not afford the payment required to cast a ballot.

Mississippi had elected African Americans to public office during Reconstruction. In the first elections after the Civil War, it had even sent H. R. Revels to the U.S. Senate. By the twentieth century, however, so few African Americans were allowed to vote that whites occupied every local and state office. The South was also rigidly segregated. Whites and African Americans had to attend separate schools, play in separate parks, go to separate churches, drink from separate water fountains, eat at separate restaurants, sit in separate bus and railroad seats, be treated in separate hospitals, and even be buried in separate cemeteries. These barriers were erected by state laws.

Economically, African Americans were also on the bottom rung of the ladder. Most of them lived in rural areas and were still doing backbreaking work as tenant farmers. Their land was owned by whites who, in theory, leased it to them for a percentage of the harvest. These owners also doled out all the necessities—from seeds and agricultural implements to clothes and basic food—to their tenants (also known as share-croppers) on credit. No matter how good the harvest, it rarely sufficed to pay off the previous year's debts. There were few possible ways to escape the misery of sharecropping.

During World War I, African-American men joined the armed forces, and some of them fought valiantly, despite continuing segregation of their units. When the war ended, African-American veterans were reluctant to return to the rural South, where 90 percent of the African American pop-ulation lived until 1910. Between 1910 and 1920, one million African Americans joined the "great migration" north.[8] They fled the cotton fields of Mississippi and Alabama, where the boll weevil had been destroying their crops and the floods of 1915 threatened their liveli-hood. They were attracted to Northern cities by factory jobs. Recruiters paid their fares, but their white coworkers often met them with hostility and kept them out of their trade unions. A wave of urban riots in the North crested in 1919.

Neshoba County, where the crime took place, consisted largely of farmland. Most of the African-American residents were the descendants of sharecroppers.

Klan Revival

Meanwhile, in both the North and the South, the KKK was revived after World War I, supposedly as a fraternal group of "white, native-born, Anglo-Saxon Protestants."[9] In 1915, *Birth of a Nation,* a popular Hollywood movie, glorified the Klansmen and ridiculed the freed slaves during Reconstruction. The ranks of the KKK swelled into millions by the 1920s. Ten thousand Klansmen marched on Washington, D.C. They controlled state governments not only in the South but also in Northern states such as Oregon and Indiana. Their political presence was also felt in New York, New Jersey, and Pennsylvania. Lynchings, in which white mobs disfigured and murdered African Americans for some rumored misdeed, had claimed over one hundred victims a year in the 1870s by the KKK, then by other white supremacists until 1915, and again by KKK groups afterward. (A lynching is a killing by a mob of someone who is believed to be guilty of a crime but has not had a trial.) An official count of lynchings for the entire period between 1882 and 1964, kept at Tuskegee University, shows that a total of forty-seven hundred African Americans were killed by mobs. The total of 581 murders in Mississippi during those years was the highest of any state.[10]

Klan violence in the twentieth century erupted as a way to keep Southern African Americans subservient. In this phase, however, news stories about lynchings caused a revulsion against the KKK. The level of violence declined. During the economic depression of the 1930s, membership in the KKK shrank to about a hundred thousand. Still, Klan members saw themselves as American patriots, opposed to African Americans, Jews, and Communists.

Another cycle of African American hopes and white reaction occurred during and after World War II. Again, African Americans joined the armed forces to fight for democracy and returned expecting a better life. Again, those who had been tenant farmers in the South went north to work in defense industries. This time, new unions such as the Congress of Industrial Organizations (CIO) accepted them as full members. By the end of the war, nearly one in three African Americans had left the South. The remaining ones were faced with another revival of the KKK, led by Dr. Samuel Green of Atlanta, Georgia. New recruits joined in the movement in the wake of the 1954 Supreme Court decision, *Brown* v. *Board of Education,* with its call for integrated public schools.

Defiance against the nine justices of the U.S. Supreme Court headed by Earl Warren swept the South. Opponents organized themselves into White Citizens' Councils, composed mostly of middle-class, respectable citizens. Meanwhile, the KKK attracted the more insecure unskilled workers. Robert "Tut" Patterson, a former football hero, founded the first council in rural Mississippi in his days at the state university. The councils started out as "a segregationist committee of white businessmen."[11] Within two years they had enrolled eighty-five thousand members in the state. Numerous chapters spread throughout the entire region. They had links to local and national lawmakers. In Washington, more than one hundred Southern senators and representatives signed the "Southern Manifesto," expressing their defiance of court-ordered integration in public schools.

With Southern governors and lawmakers competing in their defiance of the federal law, the reborn KKK had protective cover when it sent out its night riders to terrorize African Americans. The press failed to mention many victims of the raids. One case that *did* get national attention in August 1955 involved fourteen-year-old Emmett Till from Chicago. He was visiting relatives in Mississippi. The boy's alleged "crime" was whistling at a white woman in a grocery store. Her relatives seized Emmett from his uncle's house in the middle of the night. After a severe beating, they shot him and threw his body into the Tallahatchie River. It was found later downstream, and two white men were identified as the murderers. At their trial, a local jury found them innocent, showing once again how difficult it was to convict whites who attacked African Americans in the South.

Brown v. *Board of Education*

There was not more Klan violence in the decade following the *Brown* decision because relatively little real integration took place during that time. The Supreme Court's order to enforce the *Brown* decision used the words "with all deliberate speed." The Southern states put the emphasis on "deliberate," not on "speed." In 1964, after ten years had passed, only 2.3 percent of African-American children were attending desegregated schools in the South, virtually none in Mississippi.[12] Only then did Justice Hugo Black, writing for the Supreme Court, comment, "There has been entirely

The South made very little progress toward school integration in the ten years following Brown v. Board of Education.

too much deliberation and not enough speed."[13] State and even federal judges in the South, with only rare exceptions, would not issue orders to admit African-American children to all-white schools. Those who bucked the racism of their communities, such as Judge J. Waties Waring of South Carolina and Skelly Wright of Louisiana, were hounded out of the South because of their decisions favoring integration.[14]

President John F. Kennedy had appointed Judge W. Harold Cox as one of three federal judges in Mississippi. Senator James Eastland, chairman of the Judiciary Committee, had insisted that Cox be appointed if Kennedy wanted to have the Senate approve the appointment of Thurgood Marshall, the National Association for the Advancement of Colored People (NAACP) counsel, to the Court of Appeals for the Second Circuit. Cox had promised that he would follow the law as interpreted by the U.S. Supreme Court.[15] Yet in a suit to allow African Americans to vote, Judge Cox said on March 8, 1964, "I am not interested in whether the registrar is going to give a registration test to a bunch of niggers on a voter drive."[16]

In another such lawsuit in October 1964, Judge Cox cited Robert Hauberg, the U.S. District Attorney for the Southern District of Mississippi, for contempt of court for refusing to sign a perjury indictment against witnesses who had testified that there had been discrimination against African Americans trying to vote. Judge Cox said such witnesses must be lying. Hauberg agreed, but he said he could not prosecute them for perjury (lying) because his boss, U.S. attorney general Nicholas Katzenbach, had ordered him not to.

During the voter registration project in 1964, civil rights workers had brought dozens of volunteer attorneys along with them. Mississippi authorities had insisted that out-of-state lawyers could only appear in court together with a local lawyer. This proved nearly impossible because only four Mississippi attorneys were willing to handle such cases. Of the more than one thousand arrests of civil rights workers that summer, nearly all asked to have their cases moved to federal court, where they might have a slightly better chance at a fair trial. Judge Cox ruled that each person trying to transfer a case to his court had to submit an individual petition together with a $500 bond. These conditions of Cox were set aside on appeal to the U.S. Court of Appeals for the Fifth Circuit in April 1964.[17]

The juries that heard cases involving civil rights workers in Mississippi were clearly against the workers. Although the 1960 census showed that 42.3 percent of the state's 2,178,000 population was African-American, it was rare to have a single African-American juror called to serve. In September 1964, thirty-three people were called to a federal

A police dog attacks an African-American man during a demonstration outside the courthouse in Jackson, Mississippi, in 1961. Peaceful demonstrators were often treated brutally by police.

grand jury to hear the first indictments (formal charges) against those suspected of murdering Schwerner, Chaney, and Goodman in September 1964. Only one of them was African American, though African Americans made up one third of the people in the eight counties of this court district. That meant they really should have had eleven African-American members to be a truly representative jury.

A grand jury of about twenty members is used in federal courts. It hears a prosecutor present evidence and witnesses against a defendant in a criminal case. A majority of these jury members has to decide to issue formal charges before the case can go to trial. Under these circumstances, it was doubtful that anyone would be charged and convicted of the three murders. This grand jury failed to bring charges, reportedly by a margin of one vote.

There was a state-funded agency known as the Sovereignty Commission that kept tabs on civil rights workers and sympathizers in Mississippi from 1957 to 1973. It had files on more than eighty-seven thousand people, sometimes seeing to it that suspects lost their jobs.[18] Through the years, the agency was headed by former governors, state lawmakers, and white businessmen who were determined to maintain segregation. One of its agents examined the car that Schwerner, Chaney, and Goodman had been driving in and concluded that there was "no physical evidence that these civil rights workers have met with foul play other than the burned car, which could easily be part of a hoax."[19] With this attitude of denial among officials, it would be that much harder for the courts to find out the truth.

chapter three

ON THE TRAIL OF THE SUSPECTS

THE INVESTIGATION— How would the suspects in the murders of Chaney, Schwerner, and Goodman ever be identified? At first, it was not clear that this was a high priority, even in Washington, D.C. Director J. Edgar Hoover of the Federal Bureau of Investigation (FBI) held a press conference on November 18, 1964. He reported that out of the thousands of times that civil rights workers had been attacked and harassed in Mississippi, the FBI had assisted in making only twenty-five arrests during the past year. But he maintained that this was not their regular job. "Over and over the FBI director emphasized that it is not his agency's business to guard anyone."[1] At other times, Hoover had indicated that he thought the civil rights movement was nothing more than a Communist plot.

Many people were shocked at Hoover's remarks. Northern newspapers, including *The New York Times* and the New York *Herald Tribune,* published editorials criticizing the failure of the

FBI to solve the murders of the three civil rights workers. They even suggested that President Johnson should fire Hoover. Among his other remarks on November 18, Hoover had called the Reverend Martin Luther King, Jr., "a notorious liar" for charging that FBI agents did not act on civil rights complaints because of their Southern sympathies. On December 2, King visited Hoover's office. They met, together with several aides of each man. The substance of the talks was never released, but King did say on leaving that Hoover had not apologized. Still, the meeting eased some of the public pressure against the FBI director.

FBI Actions

Perhaps as a result of that meeting, FBI agents arrested nineteen men in southeast Mississippi on December 4, including Sheriff Rainey and Deputy Price, on charges of

conspiracy. They were taken to the Naval Air Station in Meridian for their collective arraignment—the formal filing of charges against them. Dr. King now praised FBI Director

FBI director J. Edgar Hoover at first resisted suggestions that the FBI keep watch on Southern sheriffs and voter registrars. He eventually agreed to use FBI agents to infiltrate the Ku Klux Klan, but set up a Mississippi office only after the June 1964 murders.

Hoover, despite their past disagreement. He said, "I must commend the Federal Bureau of Investigation for the work they have done in uncovering the perpetrators of this dastardly act. It renews my faith in democracy."[2]

Case Derailed

As suddenly as the case had been brought, it turned ugly. On December 10, a preliminary hearing was held by U.S. commissioner Esther Carter, solely on the point of whether the charges should now be heard by a grand jury. When Carter asked to examine the evidence, it turned out to be just a single FBI agent's statement that he had taken down a confession from Horace Doyle Barnette, one of the defendants. That was inadmissible, she ruled, because by itself it was merely hearsay, a statement by others without the witness's own personal knowledge. In the absence of any further evidence, she had to dismiss the case.

Justice Department attorney Robert Owen did not want to reveal the entire case at this early stage. If he listed other witnesses, they might be intimidated before the trial even started. He telephoned his boss, Attorney General Nicholas Katzenbach, and then pulled the government's case out of the preliminary hearing. The defendants congratulated each other. Later in the day, the Justice Department issued a statement, declaring that "the refusal by a U.S. commissioner to accept a law-enforcement officer's report . . . in a preliminary hearing is totally without precedent."[3] However, the department asked Federal District Judge W. Harold Cox to reconvene the federal grand jury as soon as possible. It would resubmit the charges when it had more of a case than just one reported confession.

A month later, on January 16, 1965, newspapers announced that the FBI was once more about to arrest Sheriff Lawrence Rainey, Deputy Cecil Price of Neshoba County, and sixteen others on charges of violating the civil rights of Schwerner, Chaney, and Goodman by killing them. Two of the earlier defendants, who had been charged with merely failing to disclose information, were now dropped from the case. One new defendant was added: Philadelphia police officer Richard Willis, who witnessed the arrest of the civil rights workers on June 21 and, later that night, accompanied Price to the city limits where the three were released.

Instead of criticism, the newspapers now directed praise at the FBI and the Justice Department. Sheriff Rainey said that he hoped that federal officers would let him surrender quietly: "If we knew just where they wanted us we'd go to the United States Commissioner's office and be waiting for them." But the sheriff grumbled that the FBI would probably "make a big production out of the case; it seems to be what they want."[4]

Indictments Issued

This time, indictments were issued by a federal grand jury, with Judge William Harold Cox presiding. Judge Cox thanked the jury for "an outstanding job. You obviously have been very conscientious and sincere in the performance of your work."[5] The jury, composed of twenty-two white members and one African-American member, issued formal criminal charges after hearing ten witnesses.

Evidently, a key to the case was testimony from two of the suspects, Horace Doyle Barnette and James Jordan, both of whom confessed their part in the crimes to the FBI. Barnette, age twenty-five, was a meat truck driver who had moved to Cullen, Louisiana; Jordan, thirty-eight, was a construction worker and an admitted KKK member living in Atlanta, Georgia. Their statements were the main pieces of new evidence since September 1964, when the same jury had failed to indict the suspects.

Assistant U.S. Attorney General John Doar was present to hear the jury's report. He was interested in having a trial

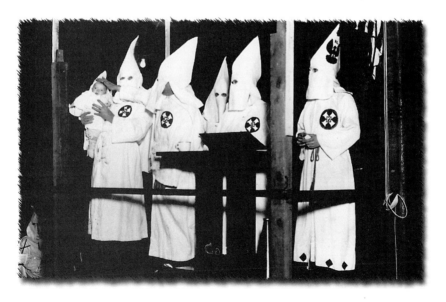

Members of racist organizations such as the Ku Klux Klan became violent in their efforts to stop the progress African Americans were making through the civil rights movement. Many of the suspects in the murders were known to be KKK members.

of the suspects in federal district court within the month. If he waited, a grand jury in Neshoba County could indict the men for the actual murder of Schwerner, Chaney, and Goodman, since state rather than federal law covered murder. Given the failure of any Mississippi jury to convict a white defendant for a crime against civil rights workers, this looked like a lost cause. Chances for a conviction were much better in federal court. But the charges were comparatively minor under two sections of a law from Reconstruction days known as the Ku Klux Klan Act: first, for the felony of conspiring (plotting) to deprive citizens of their rights; second, for the misdemeanor of law enforcement officers inflicting "summary punishment"—such as murdering the three civil rights workers—without due process of law.

All eighteen men were taken to Esther Carter, the U.S. commissioner, who typed out the formal charges against them. Under the court's rules, she had to see the men "in reasonable time" to set bail for their release until they were tried. Sheriff Rainey and Deputy Price first had to surrender their sidearms to a federal marshal in the courthouse at Philadelphia. Then they joined the other defendants who had been picked up earlier. These included Jimmy Lee Townsend, a seventeen-year-old high school dropout; Billy Wayne Posey, age twenty-eight, who ran a filling station where Townsend worked; Jerry McGrew Sharpe, twenty-one, another high school dropout; and Edgar Killen, a thirty-nine-year-old fundamentalist preacher at two small rural churches. Killen also owned a sawmill.

The grand jury disclosed its version of the crime: Deputy Price had released the three prisoners, who were returning to Meridian when they were intercepted by a lynch mob at about 10:30 P.M. on June 21, 1964. Price stopped them about nine miles south of Philadelphia. He put them into a sheriff's car and drove them down a lonely side road, where they were murdered. Then Posey took the bodies to an earthen dam several miles away, where a bulldozer covered them with tons of red clay soil. They were not found until August 4 after an intensive search. The lynch mob had included Price, Posey, Townsend, Sharpe, Jimmy Snowden, Jordan, Jimmy Arledge, Alton Wayne Roberts, E.G. ("Hop") Barnett, and Horace Doyle Barnette, along with eight others.[6] After their arraignment, Rainey and Price joked with friends until all the defendants were released by Commissioner Carter on $5,750 bond each.

A reporter who visited Philadelphia, the scene of the murders, reported that in January 1965, not much had changed since the previous June. The KKK had sent out its annual Christmas greetings. They contained an attack on Jews, who were called "not a religious organization [but] a cult of liars and murderers which is centuries old." This was followed by an anti-Catholic statement: "True Christians will waste little time or effort in attacking the Roman Papacy or any other false-Christ for their many obvious frauds."[7]

In the African-American section of town, one woman said that she doubted a Mississippi jury could be found to convict the killers of Chaney, Schwerner, and Goodman: "I [haven't] got much confidence in Mississippi doing anything right." An African-American delegation had visited Washington and told a Justice Department official, "We didn't have no roads, no law, no mail service." The official replied that conditions would be "something better in the future."[8] Still, a white clergyman, pastor of a Baptist Church, said he believed anyone found guilty should be punished according to the law. Would a jury really convict them? "Many of our people would be embarrassed and ashamed if convictions do not follow conclusive evidence," answered the Reverend Roy Collum.[9]

Federal Court or State Court?

Did the federal government have a right to try the men for civil rights violations when the real charge was murder? On January 22, lawyers for seven of the eighteen defendants argued before Judge Cox in federal district court that this was the wrong place for their trial. If their alleged crime was murder, it had to be tried in a state court. The only time that murder can be tried in federal court, they said, is when it is committed on federal property, such as in a military camp.[10] The defense lawyers filed other papers, including a motion that the suspects be tried separately. Each of them, they said, was "entitled to his own day in court."[11] If they were tried together, they would not get a fair trial, the lawyers claimed, because the jury would be prejudiced when it heard the two confessions.

Four days later, on January 26, Judge Cox surprised the defense attorneys during a hearing on their motion for separate trials. He announced that James Edward Jordan was

Mrs. Beulah Melton, wife of a shooting victim, is interviewed by NAACP field secretary Medgar W. Evers. Evers was himself murdered by a sniper on June 12, 1963. Many African Americans were doubtful that the killers of the three civil rights workers would be brought to justice.

going to plead either guilty or "no contest" to the federal conspiracy charges against him at his trial in Atlanta. One of the attorneys, in turn, had a surprise of his own. He said that Horace Doyle Barnette now claimed that he had been coerced into making his confession to the FBI. Barnette was, therefore, withdrawing the alleged statement.[12] Judge Cox ruled that Jordan and Barnette would be tried separately from the sixteen others. He had not yet decided the other requests made by the defendants—for removal of their cases to a state court and for individual trials for each of them.

The next day, January 27, the remaining defendants all pleaded not guilty to the federal charge of conspiracy to murder the three civil rights workers the previous June 21. This time, Judge Cox said that he would need another two weeks to rule on the defense motions.[13] During the noon recess, Alton Wayne Roberts, one of the defendants, attacked a Columbia Broadcasting System cameraman on the courthouse lawn. While a city police officer looked on, Roberts kicked and struck the cameraman, who later needed six stitches to close the wound over his eye. Other photographers took pictures of the attack, but Sheriff Rainey said it was the fault of photographers who "are always causing trouble."[14] In the afternoon session, the defendants argued that the FBI had violated the Fourth Amendment prohibition against unreasonable search and seizure when agents had dug up the bodies of Schwerner, Chaney, and Goodman on August 4. The agents, however, testified that they had given a search warrant to Olen Burrage, a defendant who owned the property, before they brought in the bulldozer. A defense lawyer argued that three days before that search, agents had come to look around, which made it an improper search. Assistant U.S. Attorney General Doar, however, cited precedents (previous court decisions) that allowed inspection by law officers of an open field even without a warrant.

Proceed in Federal Court?

On February 25, Judge Cox was ready to rule on whether the case could proceed in federal court. To a surprised courtroom, the judge announced that he was dismissing felony indictments against seventeen of the eighteen defendants.[15] That meant that all of them—except James Jordan, who was going to be tried separately in the Atlanta federal court—could be tried only for a misdemeanor rather than a serious crime. The original charges were based on two civil rights laws passed by Congress during Reconstruction. Section 241, originally passed as the 1870 Enforcement Act (also known as the Ku Klux Klan Act), later part of the 1871 Civil Rights Act, enforced the Fourteenth Amendment, by protecting the rights of citizens against state action. Section 242, derived from the 1866 Civil Rights Act, enforced the Thirteenth Amendment abolishing slavery. It was designed to prevent new restrictions, such as the Black Codes, to limit the rights of former slaves. Under the first section, the defendants were accused of plotting the murders of Schwerner, Chaney, and Goodman, thereby depriving them of their constitutional rights. Under the second, they were accused of depriving the victims of their rights "under color of law," implying actions by state officials. The maximum sentence under Section 241 was ten years' imprisonment and a $5,000 fine for a felony conviction. Under Section 242 it was one year's imprisonment and a $1,000 fine for a misdemeanor. These laws had been rarely used at that time. But until Congress passed a new comprehensive civil rights act, they were the only way for the federal government to protect African Americans in the South from attacks by extremists.

Judge Cox had been known during his three years as a federal district judge for closely following points of legal procedure.[16] But he had also made it clear that he was not in favor of lawyers who came before him to argue antisegregation cases. He had written to John Doar of the Justice Department during *United States* v. *Mississippi,* a 1963 voting rights case: "I spend most of the time fooling around with lousy cases brought before me by your department in the civil rights field, and I do not intend to turn my docket over to your department for your political advancement."[17] In reducing and dismissing charges against the defendants accused of murdering Schwerner, Chaney, and Goodman, he referred to a case decided by the Supreme Court in 1951.

People all over the country reacted to the news of the civil rights struggle in the South. Here, students from CORE and SNCC chain themselves to a federal courthouse in New York City to protest civil rights abuses in Jackson, Mississippi, in 1965.

In that case, *United States* v. *Williams,* the justices had split 5-4.[18] The *Williams* case concerned a private detective with a special police officer's badge, who had beaten robbery suspects until they confessed. The opinion, written by Justice Felix Frankfurter, said that the 1870 law had not been intended to cover conspiracies by state officials and others unless they were clearly acting "under color of law." According to Frankfurter, Congress could protect such rights of citizens as voting in congressional elections when individuals or state officials interfered with them; however, it could not protect other rights that the Constitution had guaranteed previously against state action.[19] That included the right of suspects to be tried under "due process of law," as stated in the Fifth Amendment, rather than being beaten (or even killed) by a police officer. Such rights would have to be asserted in state, not federal, court.

The second precedent cited by Judge Cox was a decision in which federal district judge W. A. Bootle threw out an indictment by the Justice Department against Ku Klux Klansmen accused of murdering Lemuel Penn, a Washington, D.C., educator, by shooting him on a Georgia highway in July 1964. Penn, a lieutenant colonel in the army reserve, had been returning from training at Fort Benning, Georgia, when the Klansmen spotted his car on a deserted road at night. Since the accused men were not connected with the state government, Judge Bootle said, they could not be charged with depriving Penn of his civil rights "under color of law." His court was not the proper place for such a trial, he said, because "the enforcement of general criminal laws is a local matter."[20]

Would Defendants Even Stand Trial?

Would the defendants in Mississippi get away without a trial for murdering the three young civil rights workers? On February 26, it appeared that a trial even on misdemeanor charges would be held for only the three law officers— Sheriff Rainey, Deputy Price, and Philadelphia policeman Richard A. Willis. Judge Cox said only they could be charged with acting "under color of law" in depriving Schwerner, Chaney, and Goodman of the rights guaranteed them by the Fourteenth Amendment.[21] The remaining defendants could be tried, he said, only on one count of conspiracy, which seemed meaningless because the three other counts relating to the murders had been dropped by the court. Judge Cox also ruled that the FBI search for the bodies had been conducted under a proper search warrant. His decision was hardly a victory for the prosecution, since the maximum sentence for the three accused law officers, if they were convicted, would be only a year in jail and a $1,000 fine for taking part in a triple murder.

This evoked an angry response from civil rights leaders. James Forman, executive director of the SNCC, said, "This is simply another manifestation of Judge Cox's consistent disregard for the rights of civil rights workers."[22] Roy Wilkins, executive director of the NAACP, said he was "mad as hell" at Judge Cox's ruling. He added that he hoped the Justice Department would appeal the decision because since his appointment in 1961, Judge Cox had never made anything but anti–civil rights rulings.[23] Fannie Lee Chaney, James Chaney's mother, said that the legal outcome was "sad for the State of Mississippi."[24]

Justice Department lawyers decided to appeal Judge Cox's rulings, even though there had never been a conviction under the two federal laws in Mississippi. They applied directly to the United States Supreme Court, which in rare cases "of imperative public importance," can hear a case directly from a district court without having the U.S. Court of Appeals rule on it first. Even if the Supreme Court reversed the district court and ordered the trial to go forward, chances seemed slim that a locally based judge and jury would convict defendants linked to the KKK. The only alternative, a trial in state court on a murder charge, appeared even more hopeless. Mississippi officials, from the governor down, had been outspoken against following any guidance from Washington. They would probably reject any evidence offered by the FBI or the Justice Department. At that time, it could spell political suicide for Southern officials to side with the civil rights movement.

chapter four

THE ROAD TO JUSTICE

WASHINGTON, D.C.— Unless the Supreme Court gave the green light to go ahead, it did not seem likely that the murderers of Chaney, Schwerner, and Goodman would ever be tried in court. Would the Court even agree to hear this case?

Supreme Court Agrees to Hear Appeal

On April 26, 1965, the Justice Department received the first piece of good news in its efforts to bring the suspected murderers to justice. The Supreme Court had agreed to hear an appeal to Judge Cox's rulings that had left only three defendants in the case charged with misdemeanors. The justices would now decide whether federal rather than state courts were the right place to try the Mississippi defendants.

The outcome of this trial would also affect what happened in three other cases.[1] The first concerned the Klansmen in Georgia accused of killing Colonel Penn in July 1964; the second involved attackers in Alabama who had bludgeoned to death James Reeb, a white Unitarian minister from Boston who had joined Martin Luther King's march from Selma to Montgomery, Alabama, on March 6, 1965; and the third involved the fatal drive-by shooting of Viola Liuzzo, a Detroit housewife. Liuzzo had given rides to demonstrators between Selma and Montgomery on March 25, 1965. Prosecution in these federal cases was directed by John Doar, who had succeeded Burke Marshall as assistant attorney general for civil rights of the Justice Department in December 1964.

Without such experienced and determined prosecutors, cases were likely to be derailed in state courts. This was demonstrated when Collie Leroy Wilkins, Jr., was tried for Liuzzo's murder in an Alabama court. The defense attorney for Wilkins, Matt Murphy, Jr., tried to ruin the reputation of not only Liuzzo but also of Gary Rowe, the FBI informer who had identified Wilkins as the killer.

Murphy described Rowe as a person who "would accept money from the Communists, money from the NAACP, money from the Martin Luther King outfit." He asked the jury, "Could you believe him on oath when you know he's a liar and a perjurer?"[2] The district attorney scarcely objected to this attack. The jury found Wilkins not guilty.

The Warren Court

Chief Justice Earl Warren headed the Supreme Court that would hear the Mississippi case. Warren and associate justices Hugo Black, William Douglas, and Tom Clark were on the court that had ruled unanimously in the 1954 case of *Brown* v. *Board of Education* to overturn racial segregation in public schools.[3] In *Cooper* v. *Aaron,* these four justices had joined with justices John Harlan, William Brennan, Felix Frankfurter, Charles Whittaker, and Potter Stewart to tell Governor Orval Faubus of Arkansas that he had to let African-American students attend Little Rock High School in 1958.[4] Now, in 1965, two of the associate justices had been replaced, but it was unlikely that the latest additions— middle-of-the-road Byron R. White and more liberal Abe

The Supreme Court that unanimously reinstated the charges in United States v. Price et al. *on March 28, 1966. (Seated, left to right) Tom Clark, Hugo L. Black, Chief Justice Earl Warren, William O. Douglas, John M. Harlan; (standing) Byron R. White, William J. Brennan, Jr., Potter Stewart, Abe Fortas.*

Fortas—would be any less open to expanding the scope of civil rights than their colleagues had been.

On November 9, the Supreme Court heard arguments in the appeal brought by the Justice Department to Judge Cox's dismissal of most charges against the defendants in the killing of the three civil rights workers. The senior lawyer for the government was Thurgood Marshall, recently appointed by President Lyndon B. Johnson to be Solicitor General, the chief attorney for the executive branch. Marshall had headed the NAACP legal staff, winning twenty-nine victories in cases heard by the Supreme Court. His most famous one was in *Brown* v. *Board of Education,* the decision in which the court had ruled that "separate but equal" was a formula inherently unequal and unconstitutional. In 1961, Marshall had been appointed by President John F. Kennedy to be a judge on the United States Court of Appeals for the Second Circuit. After four years as a distinguished jurist in that post, he had become the first African-American Solicitor General of the United States. At Marshall's side was Assistant Attorney General John Doar, head of the Justice Department's civil rights division, with long experience in Mississippi and Alabama.

The Defense Team

Defending the validity of Judge Cox's rulings were some of the attorneys from Neshoba County who had been lawyers for the accused Klansmen. They included H. C. ("Mike") Watkins, Dennis Goldman, Laurel G. Weir, and Herman Alford. It might have been a more even contest if the appeal had been argued by Mississippi officials, such as the state attorney general, or by a top attorney in Washington, D.C. Still, the four Neshoba lawyers had one advantage: They had a precedent of the Supreme Court on which to rest their case. This was the *Williams* case, mentioned in the last chapter, decided by the Court only fourteen years before. The opinion for a divided court written by Justice Frankfurter had appeared to rule out using the federal civil rights laws against private persons rather than state officials. Marshall and Doar were faced with what seemed an uphill battle, convincing a majority of the justices to overturn that precedent.

The Prosecution's Plea

On November 9, 1965, Thurgood Marshall asked the Court to punish "lynch mob murder" by invoking the 1870 federal law against conspiracy in both the killing of the three civil rights workers in Mississippi and that of Lemuel Penn in Georgia.[5] He tried to persuade the justices to overturn the district court judges who had ruled that these murders could only be tried in state, not federal, court. Marshall argued that the felony provision of the 1870 law could be used against a "gang of toughs" who had denied African Americans their rights guaranteed by the Fourteenth Amendment. Specifically, he said the Mississippi murders violated the "due process" clause of that amendment, because police officers had turned Schwerner, Chaney, and Goodman over to a lynch mob. Therefore, all the defendants had engaged in the "state action" required by the law.

On the defendants' side, Mike Watkins, of Meridian, Mississippi, offered a states' rights argument. He said that the 1870 law was not intended to protect so-called natural rights of citizens, such as the right to be free from racial violence. These basic rights may be protected only by the states. Section 241, he concluded, could be used only when "federal rights" such as voting or using the post office were violated.

The Basis for the Court's Decision

On which part of the Constitution would the Supreme Court base its decision? It could, as the defendants urged, find the key in the Tenth Amendment. That says powers not given by the Constitution to the federal government nor denied to the states are reserved to (retained by) the states or the people. It is the basis for so-called police powers, by which states regulate the age at which its residents can drive or drink, and the conduct of ordinary criminal trials. Or the Court could, as the Justice Department had argued it should, ground its opinion in the Fourteenth Amendment. A key clause here prohibits a state from depriving "any person of life, liberty and property without the due process of law." At the end of the nineteenth century, the Court had used "due process" as a means of deciding against attempts by states to regulate workers' hours or the price of goods because it threatened property rights. This "substantive" use of due process was seen at the time as a way for judges to read their own economic views into the Constitution. So, more recently, the Court had shifted to emphasizing "procedural due process," which tries to ensure that individuals are treated fairly by the government. In the

Mississippi case, that meant determining if officials had dealt in legal ways with Schwerner, Chaney, and Goodman.

Another key clause of the Fourteenth Amendment does not let states deny "any person . . . the equal protection of the laws." Under the New Deal of the 1930s, the Court had broadened the scope of economic activities that could be regulated by Congress. More recently, it had extended the "equal protection" clause to the rights of African-American students to attend public schools. Under the Warren Court, more and more rights previously left to states to provide (or not, as they saw fit)—such as whether to supply an attorney to a defendant in a criminal case—were given blanket protection under federal law.[6]

United States v. Price et al.

On March 28, 1966, the Supreme Court announced its decision in *United States* v. *Price et al.*[7] The opinion was written by Justice Abe Fortas, who had taken his seat on the Court on October 4, 1965, just a month before the appeal had been argued. Fortas had come to Washington as a Yale Law School graduate in 1933 and had worked in various government posts before joining a successful law firm. Among his legal successes was arguing the 1963 case of *Gideon* v. *Wainwright,* which established the right to a lawyer of anyone accused of a crime in a state court. Fortas had won the friendship of Lyndon B. Johnson in 1948 when he defended the then senator's disputed primary election victory. In 1965, President Johnson chose his trusted friend and adviser to serve on the Supreme Court.

Supreme Court Justice Abe Fortas wrote the opinion in United States v. Cecil Price et al.

Justice Fortas narrowed the case to a single issue: Did the Reconstruction-era laws cover the crimes of which the eighteen defendants were accused? He dealt first with Section 242, the 1866 law that made it a misdemeanor to "willfully subject" anyone to deprivation of their "rights, privileges and immunities secured or protected by the Constitution or laws of the United States." Judge Cox, Fortas said, had correctly found that the three law officers had acted "under color of law" by conspiring against Chaney, Schwerner, and Goodman. Cox was wrong, however, in dismissing charges against the fifteen other "private persons" who were accused of participating in the crime. Even if they were not law officers, these men were part of "the brutal joint adventure" that ended with the triple murder. In taking the lives of the three young men, the killers were also depriving them of their constitutional "rights, privileges and immunities," specifically, of "due process of law." In other words, if the three civil rights workers had done something wrong they could be punished only by a proper arrest, trial, and judgment, not by a lynch mob that acted outside the law.[8]

Deputy Sheriff Price (left) and Sheriff Rainey shown at their arraignment.

"Under Color of Law"

Judge Cox had made a sharp distinction between the state and local police who were acting "under color of law" and the fifteen other defendants who were "private individuals." Justice Fortas found that distinction to be "in error." He said the police and the others in the mob had acted hand in glove. The 1866 federal law covered their joint action or conspiracy:

> Private persons, jointly engaged with state officials . . . are acting "under color" of law for purposes of the statute. To act "under color" of law does not require that the accused be an officer of the State. It is enough that he is a willful participant in joint activity with the State or its agents. . . . The brutal joint adventure was made possible by state detention and calculated release of the prisoners by an officer of the State. . . . [It] was part of the monstrous design described by the indictment. State officers participated in every phase of the alleged venture: the release from jail, the interception, assault and murder. It was a joint activity, from start to finish. Those who took advantage of participation by state officers in accomplishment of the foul purpose alleged must suffer the consequences of that participation. . . . They were participants in official lawlessness . . . and hence under color of law.[9]

Fortas still had to dispose of the *Williams* decision on which Judge Cox had relied to dismiss felony charges against all of the defendants. As was pointed out in the last chapter, the justices had split 5-4 in that case. Justice Black had voted with those who did not think the 1870 law covered conspiracies to injure persons exercising their Fourteenth Amendment rights. Now Fortas pointed out that Black had not explicitly agreed with that interpretation of the law. Black, he said, had not really spelled out his reasons for holding back. He had just said that a competent court had already decided the issue. An earlier trial had already thrown out the conspiracy charges against Williams and the other defendants. Therefore, whether Section 241 could be read as protecting due process of law was "still an open question," according to Fortas.[10]

The problem with this reading by Fortas of the *Williams* decision was that Black was right there on the present Court.

And he evidently disagreed with Fortas on the meaning of his vote in 1951. While Black went along with the Court majority now in the Mississippi case, he only concurred. That is, he voted with the other justices to try the eighteen defendants in federal court. But he did not go along with the part of the opinion in which Fortas was interpreting the *Williams* opinion, though he did not spell out why.

Fortas, however, had three other ways to get around any precedent set by *Williams*. First, he found an earlier decision by Justice Oliver Wendell Holmes to follow. In deciding a case of voter fraud, this great justice, who served from 1902 to 1932, had said that Section 241 deals with "Federal rights and all Federal rights." It was designed as a response by the nation, Holmes said, to "doings of the Ku Klux Klan"; their "acts of violence obviously were in the minds of Congress."[11] Holmes, who had been a Union officer during the Civil War, became known for his forceful dissents on the Court, especially in cases about free speech and other civil liberties, including the victims of lynching.[12] Holmes's "broad" reading of the law, said Fortas, was justified. The law had been passed after several years of "continued denial of rights to Negroes, sometimes accompanied by violent assaults."[13]

Besides this rather obscure opinion of Holmes's, Fortas also found a broad view of Section 241 justified by its history. The author of that 1870 law was a Senator Poole of North Carolina. He told the Senate that it was needed because Southern states were undermining the Fourteenth and Fifteenth amendments. Poole said that Section 241 was written to punish individuals behind such actions, whether or not they were state agents: "It matters not whether those individuals be officers or whether they are acting upon their own responsibility."[14]

The third point of Fortas was to argue that, regardless of whether Frankfurter had been right in barring federal action in the *Williams* case, times had changed since 1951. In the earlier period it was rare to have the federal government protect individual rights from the states. Now, however, a federal role was accepted in many areas, such as "the freedom to travel, nondiscriminatory access to public areas and … educational facilities." This was a way of indicating the impatience of the Court with Southern delays in school integration following the 1954 *Brown* decision. It also recognized that in 1964 Congress had passed a strong civil rights act, which let federal officials enforce voting rights, school integration, equal employment opportunities, and the desegregation of public accommodations such as restaurants, parks, and hotels. With that new balance in state-federal relations, it was right for the Court, Fortas said, "to punish denials by state action of [a person's] constitutional rights."[15]

A unanimous Supreme Court, therefore, sent the case back to Judge Cox's district court. The defendants would have to face all the original charges.

chapter five

THE CIVIL RIGHTS TRIAL IN MERIDIAN

COURTHOUSE—The trial in federal district court was scheduled to start on October 7, 1966. Before it could begin, however, the defense lawyers were able to force another delay. In a strange twist for attorneys defending segregationists, they filed a motion protesting the way that the grand jury had been chosen. The members had been picked from a jury pool that did not have the number of African Americans, Native Americans, and women proportional to their number in the local population.

Federal prosecutors had brought similar challenges in other cases in the South, so this time they conceded the point and waited until a new grand jury could be picked. At last, on February 28, 1967, a fresh panel met and issued a new set of indictments, or formal charges.[1] It would take another seven months for the trial to finally get under way on October 9, 1967, three years and four months after Chaney, Schwerner, and Goodman had been murdered.

Judge Cox Presides Again

The same Judge Cox who had dismissed earlier indictments presided in the courtroom. This time, he granted a key motion for the prosecution. The defense had moved to have the jury drawn from the six counties around Neshoba County, where the murders had taken place. Instead, Cox agreed with Assistant Attorney General Doar that the pool for jurors should stretch across the entire Southern District of Mississippi. Later Doar said, "We would never have had a chance with a jury from those counties around Neshoba."[2]

One African-American woman was excluded from the jury because she had taken part in a civil rights march. Shown is one of the demonstrators who attended the March on Washington for Jobs and Freedom in 1963.

Now it was less likely that jurors would be bound by friendship or family ties to any of the defendants or their lawyers.

The original list of two hundred prospective jurors included seventeen African Americans. All were rejected on peremptory challenges (without having to give a reason) by the defense attorneys. One African-American woman was asked if she had ever taken part in civil rights activities. Yes, she said, she was a member of the NAACP and had gone on one march. She was excused. A white man was asked if he belonged to the White Knights of the KKK. He said that he had "a couple of years ago," then denied that it would influence him as a juror. He was not excused for "cause," but he was not picked for the trial jury of twelve.[3] The final panel consisted of five men and seven women, all of whom were white. Doar later said he was looking for those with signs of intelligence and those whom his staff had found to have well-kept homes.

Some of the defendants indicted in December 1964 had been dropped and others added. For example, teenager Jimmy Lee Townsend and seventy-four-year-old Otha Neal Burkes were out because the prosecution saw that there was not enough evidence to win a conviction. Newly indicted were Sam Bowers, the imperial wizard of the KKK, and E. G. ("Hop") Barnett, former sheriff of Neshoba County. The new indictment listed Deputy Sheriff Price and eight others as participants in the killings. The rest were listed as having taken unspecified parts.

Prosecution's Opening Statement

In his opening statement, Doar told the jury that the defendants had plotted to murder Schwerner, Chaney, and Goodman because "they didn't like what these boys stood for." Then he explained why a federal rather than a state court was needed to address the crime.

> I am here because your National Government is concerned about your local law enforcement. . . . When local law enforcement officials become involved as participants in violent crime and use their position, power and authority to accomplish this, there is very little to be hoped for, except with assistance from the Federal Government. . . . [This] means only that these defendants are tried for a crime under Federal law in a Mississippi city, before a Mississippi federal judge, in a Mississippi courtroom before twelve men and women from the State of Mississippi.[4]

Doar was trying to overcome the negative feeling in this region against the federal government.

Defense's Opening Statement

One of the twelve defense lawyers tried to use this bias against the federal government to his advantage. In his opening argument, he said that Doar, the lead prosecutor, was the same spokesperson for the Justice Department who had "forced the Negro James Meredith into the University of Mississippi."[5] Doar merely nodded his head in acknowledgment. He was waiting for the defense to go too far. That happened after Doar presented his first witness, the Reverend Charles Johnson of Meridian, who had worked with Schwerner in 1964. During cross-examination, defense attorney Laurel Weir began by asking whether Schwerner had spoken against the Vietnam War, burned his draft card, or been an atheist. Johnson said no. Then Weir asked him if Schwerner had tried to get "young male Negroes to sign" a pledge to rape a white woman once a week during the summer of 1964.[6]

At that point, Judge Cox broke in. He told Weir that he considered this question "highly improper," unless the defense could show "a good basis for it." When Weir said someone had passed him the question, Cox persisted, asking, "Who is the author of that question?" Herman Alford, one of the other defense attorneys, said Edgar Killen "wrote the question." Cox responded, "I'm not going to allow a farce to be made of this trial. I don't understand such a question as that and I don't approve. If there's no basis to it I'm going to have something to say about it when we get through."[7] It was clear that, this time, Judge Cox was not exhibiting the racism he had been criticized for in earlier cases. Perhaps he was reacting to the angry senators who had once urged that he be impeached for making derogatory remarks about African-American plaintiffs.

Later, Doar called the provocative defense question "a tremendous blunder" and a "big turning point" in the trial. No longer could the defendants assume that they would be automatically acquitted, as previous white attackers of African Americans and of civil rights workers had been in Mississippi. Doar said, "Cox made it clear that he was taking the trial seriously. That made the jurors stop and think: 'If Judge Cox is taking this stand, we'd better meet our responsibility as well.' "[8] The jurors included housewives, a secretary, factory workers, and a grocery store owner. During the eleven days of the trial, the judge allowed them to go home at night as long as they did not discuss the case.

The Prosecution's Case

The prosecution began by having witnesses establish the facts of the murder. Then John Doar got to the heart of his case—the three informers who had witnessed the crime and a fourth who had withdrawn his confession afterward. An FBI expert first described the discovery of the three bodies "deep within the earthen dam of a farm pond."[9] Despite defense objections, Judge Cox allowed him to show photographs. The judge conceded that they did "present some gruesome details," but he refused to declare a mistrial, as the defense had asked. Another FBI agent testified that he had found the burned-out station wagon, with its clock stopped at 12:45 A.M.—the time that it had been set afire. Then Dr. William Featherstone described the bullets he had found when he examined the bodies of the men—three in Chaney's body, one each in Schwerner's and Goodman's.

Three other witnesses set the times surrounding the crime. Ernest Kirkland told how he had seen Schwerner, Chaney, and Goodman drive off after they had discussed the recent firebombing of the Mount Zion Church the afternoon of their disappearance. Minnie Herring, wife of the Neshoba County jailer, said that she had seen the three men released at 10:30 P.M. on June 21, 1964, six hours after Deputy Price had brought them in. An African-American man who lived in nearby Kemper County said that he had been driving to his night-shift job at 1:30 A.M. the next day when he saw a vehicle burning on the spot where the station wagon was later found.[10]

The first of the Klansmen to become a prosecution witness was Sergeant Carlton Wallace Miller of the Meridian police. He recalled how he had been recruited into the KKK in April 1964 by Edgar Ray Killen, a fundamentalist Baptist minister.[11] Later that month, Miller had attended a KKK meeting where members discussed plans to "whip" Michael Schwerner. Miller identified eleven of the defendants as having been present at that meeting. They were told that Schwerner's "elimination" had been approved by Samuel H. Bowers, the imperial wizard of the Klan for the state. A week after the three had disappeared, Killen told Miller that the three "had been shot and were dead," buried fifteen feet underground in a dam. Miller said that he spent "many, many" restless nights before he decided to testify. He admitted that he had been paid $2,400 by the FBI for travel and other expenses, "as a man, not as an officer."[12]

James Jordan was scheduled to testify next. He had been flown back to Meridian from his new home in Georgia. On October 11, five men with drawn guns escorted him into the courtroom. There was a shock as Jordan collapsed with severe chest pains. He was rushed to a hospital, where he was diagnosed as having hyperventilated. He was not seriously ill.

The next afternoon, Doar called Jordan as a witness. Jordan looked exhausted and spoke in a quiet voice. He told

A stained glass window honoring James Chaney, Michael Schwerner, and Andrew Goodman is in Sage Chapel at Cornell University, which Schwerner attended.

of a KKK meeting in Meridian at 6:00 P.M. on June 21, 1964. Preacher Killen "said he had a job he needed some help with over in Neshoba County. He said that two or three of those civil rights workers were locked up and they needed their rear ends tore up."[13] Killen said he needed six or seven men for the job, and Jordan began rounding them up. A dozen volunteers showed up to meet with Killen in the early evening. He took them to wait at an old warehouse on the edge of Philadelphia. The two carloads of Klansmen were told by a police officer who drove by to head for Highway 19 in the direction of Meridian. One of the cars broke down, but the other, driven by Jordan, soon found Deputy Sheriff Price's patrol car, red light blinking, as it pulled a station wagon off the road.

Price told Schwerner, Chaney, and Goodman to get in the back of his car. The Klansmen's car followed to a deserted stretch of Rock Cut Road. There, Jordan claimed, he became a lookout. He heard four shots but did not see the actual killings—just the three bodies lying beside the road later. Jordan identified seven of the defendants who had been at the murder scene: Deputy Price, Jimmy Arledge, Horace Barnette, Billy Wayne Posey, Alton Wayne Roberts, Jerry Sharpe, and Jimmy Snowden. They wore gloves while they removed all traces of the shooting. Then the bodies of the three victims were taken in their station wagon to a "hollow," where a bulldozer buried them in a common grave. The station wagon was supposed to be destroyed in Alabama, but it was found in Neshoba County two days later. Jordan said that he had later agreed to tell FBI agents "everything" if they would help him to get out of town. They gave him $3,000, which he used to buy a car and move to Georgia. Until he found a new job a year later, the FBI continued to give him one hundred dollars a week.[14] Jordan's testimony was clearly crucial to the prosecution.

A third prosecution witness, the Reverend Delmar Dennis, also a member of the KKK, identified Sheriff Rainey and Deputy Price as Klan members. He, too, confirmed that Sam H. Bowers, the state Klan's imperial wizard, had approved the murder of Schwerner. Bowers had told the Neshoba KKK that Mickey Schwerner was "a thorn in the side of everyone living, especially the white people, and should be taken care of."[15] Afterward, Bowers told them they had done "a job to be proud of" and any evidence "should be gotten rid of." He also said that this "was the first time that Christians had planned and carried out the execution of a Jew."[16] Dennis showed the court a letter from Bowers that used a code of sawmill terms. For example, "the big logging operation" referred to the killings on Rock Cut Road.[17] On cross-examination, defense lawyer Weir brought up the money that Dennis had received from the FBI for his undercover work: "Instead of 30 pieces of silver, you got $15,000." Judge Cox cut him short, "If you've got any more quips like that, I'm going to let you sit down. . . . Don't ever let that happen again."[18]

The final surprise evidence by the prosecution was the confession that Horace Barnette had given to the FBI on November 20, 1964, before withdrawing it. Over defense objections, Judge Cox allowed Doar to read the document to the court, as long as the name of Alton Wayne Roberts was blanked out for legal reasons. It was a graphic account of the murders: Mickey Schwerner was pulled out of the car, spun around, and asked, "Are you the nigger lover?"

"Sir," he answered, "I know just how you feel."

"Blank" took "a pistol in his hand and shot Schwerner." The same man then took Goodman out of the car and shot him, so that he fell back toward the bank. Jordan then stepped forward and said, "Save one for me." Contradicting Jordan's testimony that he had been only a lookout, Barnette said that Jordan shot Chaney after pulling him into the road. The confession was verified by Henry Rask, an FBI agent. Rask said that Barnette said the killings "had been bothering him and he wanted to tell us about it." Barnette had accepted $300 from the FBI "for services rendered and wages lost" during a total of twenty-seven interviews.[19]

Defense Evidence

Now it was the defense's turn to offer evidence. The lawyers' strategy was to cast doubt on the truthfulness of prosecution witnesses and to offer testimony to the good character of the defendants. They also tried to establish alibis showing that these eighteen men were working, fishing, in church, attending funerals—anything but with a lynch mob at the time of the murders.[20] During Doar's cross-examination, he tried to show the bias of such witnesses for the defense, based on their family ties or joint membership in the KKK with the accused. The parade of defense witnesses took place at a fast pace, averaging seven minutes apiece. In a bizarre finale, two of the more than forty character witnesses were African Americans who said they knew Imperial Wizard Bowers but did not connect him with any KKK activities.

Prosecution's Last Word

Doar summed up the prosecution's case on October 18. He told of the events that culminated in the murders. The accused, he said, had hatched a "diabolical plot." Pointing at Deputy Price, Doar charged that Price had "used the machinery of his office—the badge, the car, the jail, the gun."[21] If the jury found the defendants not guilty, he concluded, "it would be as true to say there was no nighttime release by Cecil Price, there are no White Knights, there are no young men dead, there was no murder."[22]

Defense's Last Word

Various defense lawyers summed up their case. One said that the defendants were "as pure as the driven snow." Another claimed the prosecution was ordered from the White House for political reasons—and their witnesses just said what they had been paid to say. A third made it sound as if the civil rights workers were responsible for their own deaths: "If life in Mississippi is miserable for the agitators who come here it's because they made it that way."[23] The jury spent the afternoon of October 18 and most of the next day discussing the case. At 3:18 P.M. the next day, the jury members told Judge Cox that after nearly nine hours of deliberation, they were still deadlocked.

Donna Howell, a student volunteer bringing African Americans to register at the county courthouse in Indianola, Mississippi, is shown here being watched by an armed deputy sheriff. Many white Southerners saw the Freedom Summer volunteers as "outside agitators" who deserved any trouble they got.

The judge ordered them to "carefully re-examine and reconsider" their positions, taking "all the time you feel is necessary."[24] Then he read new instructions taken from *United States* v. *Allen,* a Supreme Court case decided in 1896.[25] The trial judge in that Arkansas case about a murder committed on an Indian reservation had persuaded a deadlocked jury to come to a unanimous verdict. Now Judge Cox repeated what has become known as the "dynamite charge" (because it breaks apart an obstruction), urging these jurors to "consult and deliberate" with open minds until they could honestly agree, even if only on a partial verdict. In the hallway afterward, a court officer reported that he had heard Alton Wayne Roberts say to Deputy Price, "Judge Cox just gave that jury a 'dynamite charge.' We've got some dynamite for 'em ourselves."[26]

Verdicts Returned

The next morning, the jury returned with seven guilty verdicts, for Deputy Sheriff Cecil Price, KKK Imperial Wizard Sam H. Bowers, Jimmy Arledge, Horace Barnette, Billy Wayne Posey, Jimmy Snowden, and Alton Wayne Roberts. Eight others were acquitted. The jury could not agree on three more—Edgar Ray ("Preacher") Killen, Jerry Sharpe, and E. G. ("Hop") Barnett, a candidate for Neshoba County sheriff. Judge Cox ordered Price and Roberts jailed without bail, because of their threat to "dynamite" the jury. He said, "There's not a power on this earth that can frighten this court. . . . We're not going to have any anarchy down here, not as long as I'm on this bench."[27] The other five men found guilty were released on $5,000 bail each. On December 29, Cox sentenced Roberts and Bowers to ten years each, Posey and Price to six years; Barnette, Snowden, and Arledge to three. All of them appealed their convictions, but the appeals failed. On March 19, 1970, five and a half years after the murders, the seven men were taken to federal prison. They were all released before serving their full term.

October 20, 1967, remains a historic day in the history of Mississippi. It was the first time that a jury convicted white men for killing African Americans or civil rights workers.

chapter six

IN THE WAKE OF "MISSISSIPPI BURNING"

REACTION—The murders of Michael Schwerner, James Chaney, and Andrew Goodman had shocked the nation. They made clear the need for strong legislation in support of civil rights. Two weeks later, on July 2, 1964, the U.S. Senate passed the bill that had been approved by the House of Representatives on February 10. This was the most comprehensive law on civil rights ever adopted by Congress. It protected the right to vote, prohibited discrimination in employment, and empow-ered the attorney general to sue for the desegregation of public facilities such as restaurants, motels, and theaters. Howard Smith, a Southern congressman, had added "sex" to the grounds (race, creed, and color) that now became illegal in discrimination against workers. He had thought that this amend-ment was so radical that it would turn his colleagues against the bill. After five congresswomen spoke in favor of including it, how-ever, the word stayed in the bill, so that women as well as African Americans won new protection of their rights.[1]

Civil Rights Laws

President Lyndon B. Johnson kept pushing for further civil rights laws. In 1965, the Voting Rights Act made illegal any "tests and devices" used by state officials against African-American voters. Federal observers and registrars would be sent to ensure fairness in registration and voting. The effects of these laws, together with the efforts of civil rights groups, had a dramatic impact in the South. In 1961, only a quarter of Southern African Americans of voting age—about 1.25

President Lyndon B. Johnson, shown here with Dr. Martin Luther King, Jr., signed the Voting Rights bill into law in 1965. Johnson did more for the rights of African Americans than any other president in the twentieth century.

million—had registered. By 1964, the total had risen to 2 million. In the next decade, another 1 million were added. As the Mississippi volunteers had hoped, now Southern candidates could no longer afford to ignore the wishes of African-American voters.[2]

The first national effort to spotlight the hurdles faced by African-American voters in Mississippi came at the Democratic party's nominating convention in August 1964, two months after the murders of the civil rights workers. The fifty thousand African Americans who had managed to enroll in Mississippi had been ignored by the all-white party organization that picked delegates who favored Barry Goldwater, a Republican senator from Arizona who was against federal civil rights laws. African-American voters, however, met in separate county conventions called by the Mississippi Freedom Democratic party (MFDP). It was a new group that supported the re-election of President Johnson. At its state meeting in Jackson, the MFDP delegates picked sixty-four African Americans and four whites pledged to Johnson. Vice-chairperson Fannie Lou Hamer presented the case for seating these loyal delegates at hearings of the credentials committee on August 22. She described how she had lost her job and been beaten by the police for her voter registration work:

> They beat me and they beat me with the long flat blackjack. I screamed to God in pain. My dress worked itself up. I tried to pull it down. They beat my arms until I had no feeling in them. After a while the first man beating my arm grew numb from tiredness.

> The other man, who was holding me, was given the blackjack. Then he began beating me. . . . All of this on account we want to register, to become first-class citizens, and if the Freedom Democratic party is not seated now, I question America.[3]

President Johnson reacted by rejecting the MFDP's claim. He did not want to risk having all delegates from the Southern states walk out of the convention. Instead, he proposed a compromise: giving two "at-large" seats to the MFDP and promising that no racially segregated delegations would be permitted in the future. Hamer and Bob Moses, the SNCC leader who had supervised Schwerner, Chaney, and Goodman, persuaded all the MFDP delegates to refuse this deal. They were able to have friendly official delegates escort them to the convention floor. As a protest, they "sat in" (illegally occupied) the official seats. But convention officials ignored them. When they left to go home, they felt betrayed by white liberals for trying to push them into an unacceptable deal.

This was one of the events that persuaded civil rights workers in the South to switch to "black power" tactics from the integrated efforts of the Freedom Summer Project. Stokely Carmichael, elected to lead the SNCC in May 1966, said that black power was "a call for black people in this country to unite, to recognize their heritage, to build a sense of community. It is a call for black people to begin to define their own goals, to lead their own organizations and to support those organizations."[4] This signaled a new turn in the civil rights struggle, abandoning the former strategy of the

Fannie Lou Hamer (under umbrella) takes part in a 1963 march for voter registration in Mississippi. Hamer was an organizer of the Mississippi Freedom Democratic Party and its spokesperson at the 1964 National Democratic Convention.

NAACP and of Martin Luther King's Southern Christian Leadership Conference (SCLC) in which African Americans had worked together with white allies.

The young leaders advocating black power soon showed that they were also impatient with the strategy of nonviolence. This occurred when James Meredith, who had integrated the University of Mississippi in 1962, began a march of 225 miles from Memphis, Tennessee, to Jackson, Mississippi, on June 5, 1966. By setting an example, Meredith hoped to encourage other African Americans to overcome their fears and register to vote.[5] But Meredith had just started his second day on Highway 51 when he was shot in the back by a Klansman who jumped out of the bushes. Meredith was wounded in the legs, neck, and back. Civil rights leaders, including Carmichael and Floyd McKissick of CORE, rushed to Memphis. The younger leaders declared that nonviolence was no longer the right way to confront Klan violence. Southern African Americans should assert their right to self-defense. The demands of African-American leaders in the late 1960s for "black power," separatism, and the right of self-defense led to a series of verbal and physical confrontations with opponents.

How had a new generation of Southerners been affected by changes in the wake of national laws and court decisions? Observers in Philadelphia, Mississippi, in 1988 found attitudes had shifted dramatically among both white and African-American residents.[6] For example, African-American customers were welcome at a new shopping mall. There were African-American officers on Philadelphia's police force. Charles Young, a local activist with the NAACP, and Aaron Henry, who had headed the MFDP, were among the state's African-American lawmakers. Deputy Sheriff Cecil Ray Price, who had returned to town after serving four years in prison, sounded regretful about past KKK violence. "I think it's better," he told an interviewer.[7] "That was a bad period. It was thrust on us all of a sudden, and we acted hastily," he said, because if society is going to be integrated, "it's better for [my son] to be brought up in it. . . . We've got to accept that this is the way things are going to

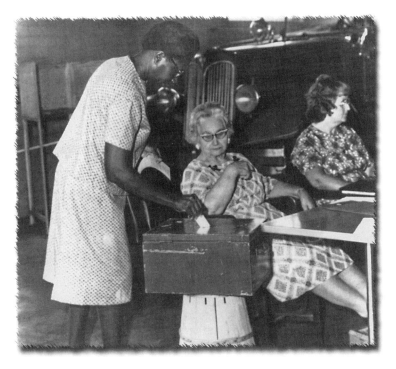

An African-American woman places her ballot in a box during congressional primary elections in Jackson, Mississippi, in June 1967. Voting rights were only part of the changes taking place in the South for African Americans.

be and that's it."[8] Price's son, Cecil, Jr., was attending the public high school rather than a segregated private school.

Many older whites who had supported the nonviolent struggle of Martin Luther King, Jr., and his circle disagreed with the more radical young activists, who were influenced by Malcolm X, an African-American Muslim leader who was assassinated on February 25, 1965. Looking back on the case he had won on behalf of the slain civil rights workers in 1967, former assistant attorney general John Doar discussed his work in Mississippi thirty years later. Doar said that he and his colleagues in the Justice Department were moved by a "philosophy grounded in hope."[9] They had responded to "the spirit of justice" at that historic moment "because it made sense," even if much of their work was stymied at first. They learned from failures, he said, since "you just got to keep going back. We couldn't change Mississippi from a desk in Washington."[10] He credits their eventual success to being seen by white Southerners as separate from the protest groups. "We didn't want white people to be able to say, 'the Civil Rights Division [of the Justice Department] and SNCC are hitched together at the hip like Siamese twins.'"As independent forces, the two groups were each able to do "what they did best."[11]

KKK Members Brought to Justice

Not only was the Klan virtually gone from Mississippi three decades after the civil rights workers were murdered, its old crimes were still being brought to justice. Samuel H. Bowers, the KKK Imperial Wizard who had ordered the three murders in 1964, was newly convicted on August 21,

1998, of a fourth murder. In a state court, he was found guilty by a jury of six whites, five African Americans, and one Asian American of ordering the killing in 1966 of Vernon Dahmer, a Hattiesburg shopkeeper who had helped African Americans register to vote. Dahmer had died when his home was firebombed.[12] Three previous trials of Bowers in state court and one in federal court had resulted in hung (undecided) juries.

In Birmingham, Alabama, Thomas E. Blanton, Jr., a former Klansman, was convicted of murdering four African-American girls in the 1963 bombing of the 16th Street Baptist Church—the atrocity that had first moved Mickey and Rita Schwerner to volunteer for the Mississippi Freedom Summer Project. Shortly after the conviction of Blanton, on May 1, 2001, prosecutors in Mississippi began reviewing the evidence used in the federal case against the murderers of Schwerner, Chaney, and Goodman in 1967. As we saw in chapter 5, the seven who were found guilty of violating the victims' civil rights received relatively light sentences. If the suspects are tried for murder in state court and convicted, they could face much heavier sentences. A second trial would not violate the Fifth Amendment rule against "double jeopardy," since the earlier charge was for a separate federal offense. But the death of Deputy Price in 2001 eliminates the need for a new trial for him.

The Mississippi attorney general finally brought a murder indictment against Edgar "Preacher" Killen in June 2005, after a group of local white and African-American businessmen campaigned to reopen the triple murder case. Witnesses had identified Killen in October 1967 as the local Klan leader who had recruited the gang of about twenty that murdered Chaney, Schwerner, and Goodman. He was acquitted in the first federal trial after the jury deadlocked 11–1; one juror later said she could never vote to convict a preacher.[13]

Samuel H. Bowers, the state Imperial Wizard of the Klan, who was serving a life term for the murder of Vernon Dahmer, had told a reporter that Killen was "getting away with murder."[14] So many years later, however, most of the witnesses from the federal trial had died or disappeared. The jurors said the evidence was insufficient for a murder conviction, but they found the eighty-year-old Killen guilty of manslaughter. Judge Marcus D. Gordon sentenced Killen to sixty years in prison: three consecutive twenty-year terms. Gordon noted, "There are three lives involved in this case, and the three lives should absolutely be respected and treated equally."[15]

Controversy Over the State Flag

There are still forces that resist change in the South today, however. In April 2001, Mississippi voters refused to give up the Confederate battle emblem as part of their state flag. The pre–Civil War elite had retaken control of the state government after the elections of 1875, and their heirs held onto power well into the twentieth century. The old emblem, added by the Reconstruction state government, symbolized Mississippi's central place among the eleven states of the Confederacy—still celebrated today by groups such as the Sons and Daughters of the Confederacy. Robert McElvaine, a local historian, argued, however, that the nostalgia of whites for the South before the Civil War should not be taken as an endorsement of the former slave system.[16] It may not make historical sense, he said, but the state's referendum showed that whites accepted the myth "that the flag does not represent slavery and hate." This subtle form of racism, he concluded, did not make Mississippi today as "different from the rest of the United States as those outside the state would like to think."[17]

In the country as a whole, observers point to the continuing existence of racial inequality. African Americans lag behind in average levels of educational achievement, health and housing, income, and wealth. Yet nearly forty years after the Mississippi Freedom Summer Project of 1964, African Americans can point to real progress. They now have growing membership in the middle class, in varied professions, and in skilled employment, as well as in government at all levels—from local school boards to the Cabinet and Supreme Court. The sacrifice of Mickey Schwerner, Andy Goodman, James Chaney, and thousands of others in the struggle for civil rights helped to pave the way to achieving equal rights for African Americans. There is still a long way to go before this goal is completely reached, but the progress made has been remarkable—especially in the South. The deaths of Schwerner, Chaney, and Goodman, and the eventual conviction of their killers, reminds us that every step forward in the civil rights movement requires united efforts among whites and African Americans.

Questions for Discussion

1. Rita and Mickey Schwerner volunteered to work for the civil rights of African Americans during the 1964 "Freedom Summer." Are there similar ways in which you could work with powerless or poor people today, after school or during vacations? How could you learn more about such opportunities?

2. A goal of the Mississippi project for student volunteers was to enable African Americans to register to vote. Since 1964, what laws and constitutional changes have made it easier for U.S. citizens to vote?

3. What additional legal changes could increase the percentage of those voting in the United States? How do some other countries achieve greater voter participation?

4. President Lyndon B. Johnson pushed for integration in such places as schools, while the governors of Southern states claimed they had the right to regulate racial relations. Can you construct arguments for both sides, basing them, respectively, on the Fourteenth and Tenth Amendments?

5. In 1964, where could a child turn if he or she were denied access to a school? Where could an adult turn if he or she was kept from registering to vote?

6. How did the Supreme Court decide the issue of trying the

suspected murderers of Schwerner, Chaney, and Goodman under federal, rather than state, law? What were the legal arguments for the prosecution and the defense? How did the Court adapt its decision to precedents (prior cases) and the 1870 law? How was the decision enforced?

7. In the mid-1960s—the period covered in this book—segregation was widespread throughout the South as well as in many other parts of the country. What racial issues divided your community, as reported by your local newspaper (in its archive or on microfilm in the library)? What specific progress has been made during the past forty years? Are you aware of remaining barriers in such fields as housing, jobs, education, or local government? How could these be overcome?

Chronology

January 1964—The Council of Federated Organizations (COFO), including the SNCC and CORE, announces the Mississippi Freedom Summer Project to register African-American voters.

February 1964—The White Knights of the Ku Klux Klan organize and, two months later, burn sixty-one crosses in various Mississippi locations.

Memorial Day 1964—Mickey Schwerner and James Chaney speak at Mount Zion Methodist Church in Neshoba County, Mississippi, urging its African-American congregation to register to vote.

June 14, 1964—CORE members Schwerner and Chaney attend a training session for summer volunteers in Oxford, Ohio, and persuade Andy Goodman to join them in Meridian, Mississippi.

June 16, 1964—Armed KKK members assault African Americans attending a meeting at Mount Zion Methodist Church. The next day the KKK burns the church to the ground—the first of twenty African American churches to be firebombed that summer. The FBI investigation is code-named MIBURN for "Mississippi Burning."

June 21, 1964—Schwerner, Chaney, and Goodman drive to Neshoba County to inspect the burned church. On their way back to Meridian, they are arrested by Deputy Sheriff Cecil Price and taken to the county jail. Price claims he released them at 10:00 P.M. The prisoners are later intercepted and murdered by the KKK.

June 22, 1964—The Justice Department orders the FBI to conduct a full-scale search for the three missing civil rights workers.

June–July 1964—The FBI interviews about one thousand residents of southeast Mississippi, half of them KKK members.

June 24, 1964—The burned-out station wagon of Schwerner, Chaney, and Goodman is found near Philadelphia, Mississippi. President Lyndon B. Johnson confers with Attorney General Robert Kennedy and others on a response to the crisis in Mississippi. The next day, the president's representative, former CIA director Allen Dulles, meets with the state's governor, Paul B. Johnson.

July 2, 1964—President Johnson signs the Civil Rights Act of 1964, the strongest law of its kind ever.

July 10, 1964—FBI director J. Edgar Hoover arrives in Jackson, Mississippi, to open a Mississippi office of the agency.

August 1964—The Mississippi Freedom Democratic Party (MFDP) challenges the all-white state delegation to the Democratic National Convention.

August 4, 1964—The bodies of Schwerner, Chaney, and Goodman are found buried in an earthen dam.

October 13, 1964—Klan member James Jordan agrees to cooperate with the FBI and confesses his part in the conspiracy.

November 19, 1964—Klan member Horace Barnette also confesses and describes the actual murders.

December 4, 1964—Nineteen members of the conspiracy, including Sheriff Rainey and Deputy Price, are arrested and charged with violating the civil rights of Schwerner, Chaney, and Goodman.

December 10, 1964—U.S. Commissioner Esther Carter dismisses charges against the nineteen on insufficient evidence.

January 1965—A federal grand jury in Jackson, Mississippi, reindicts eighteen defendants accused of civil rights violations. Horace Barnette's confession is entered into evidence.

February 25, 1965—Federal judge William Cox dismisses the indictments (except against Rainey, Price, and police officer Willis) because the other conspirators were not acting "under color of law."

April 26, 1965—The U.S. Supreme Court agrees to hear the Justice Department's appeal of Judge Cox's ruling.

November 9, 1965—The Supreme Court hears oral arguments in the case, with Solicitor General Thurgood Marshall arguing for the appeal.

March 28, 1966—The Supreme Court unanimously overrules Judge Cox and reinstates the indictments. Justice Fortas's opinion states that all eighteen were acting "under color of law."

May 1966—Stokely Carmichael, of the SNCC, urges that black power tactics of self-defense replace nonviolence.

June 6, 1966—A Klansman shoots James Meredith on the second day of his "march against fear" in Mississippi.

February 18, 1967—A federal grand jury issues new indictments against eighteen conspirators in the civil rights murders.

October 7, 1967—The trial of the Neshoba County conspirators begins. Prosecution witnesses include former Klansmen James Jordan and Delmar Dennis and Sergeant Carlton Wallace of the Meridian police.

October 18, 1967—The case goes to the jury, which is deadlocked until it is urged by Judge Cox to deliberate further.

October 20, 1967—The jury returns verdicts of guilty against seven defendants, acquits eight, and is unable to reach a verdict on three of the men charged.

December 29, 1967—Those found guilty of conspiracy are sentenced to prison for terms ranging from three to ten years.

September 1998—Imperial Wizard Sam Bowers is found guilty in the 1966 murder of Vernon Dahmer, an African-American man from Mississippi who helped other African Americans to register to vote.

April 2001—A majority of Mississippi voters decides to keep the Confederate emblem as part of the state flag.

June 2005—Edgar Ray Killen is found guilty of manslaughter in the deaths of Goodman, Chaney, and Schwerner, and is sentenced to sixty years in prison.

Chapter Notes

Chapter 1. Three Missing Civil Rights Workers

1. William Bradford Huie, *Three Lives for Mississippi* (New York: WCC Books, 1965), p. 56.

2. Ibid., p. 92.

3. William H. McIlhany, *Klandestine: The Untold Story of Delmar Dennis and His Role in the FBI's War Against the Ku Klux Klan* (New Rochelle, N.Y.: Arlington House, 1975), p. 25.

4. Douglas O. Linder, "The Mississippi Burning Trial: A Trial Account," *Famous American Trials Page,* 2000, <http://www.law.umkc.edu/faculty/projects/ftrials/price&bowers/Account.html> (August 9, 2001).

5. Claude Sitton, "U.S. Official Warns Mississippi-Bound Students," *The New York Times,* June 20, 1964, p. 12.

6. Claude Sitton, "Students Warned on Southern Law," *The New York Times,* June 19, 1964, p. 16.

7. Claude Sitton, "Students Briefed on Peril in South," *The New York Times,* June 17, 1964, p. 18.

8. Claude Sitton, "Rights Campaigners Off for Mississippi," *The New York Times,* June 21, 1964, p. 1.

9. Claude Sitton, "3 in Rights Drive Reported Missing," *The New York Times,* June 23, 1964, p. 1.

10. Huie, p. 162.

11. Mary King, *Freedom Song: A Personal Story of the 1960s Civil Rights Movement* (New York: William Morrow & Co., 1987), p. 378.

12. Sitton, "3 in Rights Drive Reported Missing," p. 1.

13. Ibid., p. 13.

14. Claude Sitton, "Rights Team's Burned Car Found in Mississippi Bog," *The New York Times,* June 24, 1964, p. 1.

15. Ibid.

16. Ibid.

17. Claude Sitton, "Hope for 3 Wanes As Dulles Opens Mississippi Talks," *The New York Times,* June 25, 1964, p. 1.

18. Rhoda L. Blumberg, *Civil Rights: The 1960s Freedom Struggle* (Boston: Twayne Publishing Co., 1991), pp. 101–102.

19. Linder.

20. Ibid.

Chapter 2. Mississippi—Civil Rights Battleground

1. Claude Sitton, "Rights Campaigners Off for Mississippi," *The New York Times,* June 21, 1964, p. 1.

2. Hodding Carter, "A Double Standard for Murder?" *The New York Times Magazine,* January 24, 1965, p. 20.

3. Ibid.

4. David M. Chalmers, *Hooded Americanism: The First Century of the Ku Klux Klan, 1865–1965* (Garden City, N.Y.: Doubleday & Co., Inc., 1965), p. 2.

5. Richard N. Current, ed., *Reconstruction (1865–1877)* (Englewood Cliffs, N.J.: Prentice-Hall, Inc., 1965), pp. 139–140.

6. C. Vann Woodward, *Reunion and Reaction: The Compromise of 1877 and the End of Reconstruction* (Boston: Little, Brown & Co., 1966), p. 8.

7. Richard Kluger, *Simple Justice: The History of* Brown *v.* Board of Education *and Black America's Struggle for Equality* (New York: Knopf, 1977), p. 67.

8. Rhoda L. Blumberg, *Civil Rights: The 1960s Freedom Struggle* (Boston: Twayne Publishing Co., 1991), p. 19.

9. Chalmers, p. 2.

10. Ernie Suggs, "Moore's Ford Lynching," *Atlanta Journal-Constitution,* March 11, 2001, p. C1.

11. Seth Cagin and Philip Dray, *We Are Not Afraid: The Story of Goodman, Schwerner, and Chaney and the Civil Rights Campaign for Mississippi* (New York: Macmillan, 1988), p. 54.

12. J. Harvie Wilkinson III, *From Brown to Bakke: The Supreme Court and School Integration, 1954–1978* (New York: Oxford University Press, 1979), p. 65.

13. *Griffin County School Board,* 377 U.S. 218.

14. Len Holt, *The Summer That Didn't End* (New York: William Morrow & Co., 1965), p. 59.

15. Cagin and Dray, p. 308.

16. Holt, p. 58.

17. *Michael Lefton et al.* v. *City of Hattiesburg,* 33F2d 280.

18. The Associated Press, "New Light Shed on Rights Story in Mississippi," *The New York Times,* January 20, 2001, p. 11A.

19. Ibid.

Chapter 3. On the Trail of the Suspects

1. Elizabeth Shelton, "Hoover in Blast at Police Corruption Opens Fire on Some Other Targets," *The Washington Post,* November 19, 1964, p. 1.

2. Walter Carlson, "Rights Leaders Hail the Arrest but Voice Doubt on Convictions," *The New York Times,* December 5, 1964, p. 18.

3. Don Whitehead, *Attack on Terror: The FBI Against the Ku Klux Klan in Mississippi* (New York: Funk & Wagnalls, 1970), p. 205.

4. Homer Bigart, "Federal Indictments Voted in 3 Mississippi Slayings," *The New York Times,* January 16, 1965, p. 1.

5. Ibid.

6. Homer Bigart, "18 Seized by U.S. in Rights Deaths," *The New York Times,* January 17, 1965, p. 6E.

7. Homer Bigart, "Eyes Still on Philadelphia," *The New York Times,* January 17, 1965, p. 6E.

8. Ibid.

9. Ibid.

10. UPI News Service, "7 Seek to Dismiss Mississippi Case," *The New York Times,* January 23, 1965, p. 18.

11. Ibid.

12. "One in Mississippi May Plead Guilty," *The New York Times,* January 27, 1965, p. 16.

13. John Herbers, "Sheriff and 16 Plead Not Guilty in Mississippi Rights Slayings," *The New York Times,* February 26, 1965, p. 1.

14. Ibid.

15. John Herbers, "U.S. Judge Voids a Major Charge in Rights Deaths," *The New York Times,* February 26, 1965, p. 1.

16. "Judge in Rights Case," *The New York Times,* February 25, 1965, p. 14.

17. Ibid.

18. *U.S.* v. *Williams,* 341 U.S. 97.

19. Fred P. Graham, "Legal Poser on Rights," *The New York Times,* February 26, 1965, p. 14.

20. Ibid.

21. John Herbers, "U.S. Judge Orders Conspiracy Trial in Rights Deaths," *The New York Times,* February 27, 1965, p. 1.

22. John Herbers, "U.S. Judge Voids a Major Charge in Rights Deaths," p. 14.

23. Ibid.

24. Ibid.

Chapter 4. The Road to Justice

1. "Court to Review 3 Rights Deaths," *The New York Times,* April 27, 1965, p. 23.

2. Seth Cagin and Philip Dray, *We Are Not Afraid: The Story of Goodman, Schwerner and Chaney and the Civil Rights Campaign for Mississippi* (New York: Macmillan, 1988), p. 442.

3. *Brown* v. *Board of Education* 347 U.S. 483.

4. *Cooper* v. *Aaron,* 358 U.S. 1.

5. Fred P. Graham, "Court Hears Rights Plea," *The New York Times,* November 10, 1965, p. 7.

6. Peter Charles Hoffer, "Due Process, Substantive," *The Oxford Companion to the Supreme Court,* Kermit Hall, ed. (New York: Oxford University Press, 1992), pp. 237–239.

7. *United States* v. *Price et al.,* 383 U.S. 787.

8. Ibid.

9. Ibid.

10. Ibid.

11. *United States* v. *Mosely,* 238 U.S. 383.

12. *Frank* v. *Mangum,* 237 U.S. 309; *Moore* v. *Dempsey,* 261 U.S. 86.

13. *United States* v. *Price et al.,* 383 U.S. 787.

14. Ibid.

15. Ibid.

Chapter 5. The Civil Rights Trial in Meridian

1. Seth Cagin and Philip Dray, *We Are Not Afraid: The Story of Goodman, Schwerner and Chaney and the Civil Rights Campaign for Mississippi* (New York: Macmillan, 1988), pp. 442–443.

2. Douglas O. Linder, "Bending Toward Justice: John Doar and the Mississippi Burning Trial," *Famous American Trials Page,* 2000, <http://www.law.umkc.edu/faculty/

projects/ftrials/trialheroes/doaressay.html> (August 9, 2001).

3. Walter Rugaber, "All-White Jury Picked as Trial of 18 in Slaying of 3 Rights Workers Begins in Mississippi," *The New York Times,* October 10, 1967, p. 21.

4. Linder.

5. Ibid.

6. Rugaber, p. 21.

7. Ibid.

8. Linder.

9. Walter Rugaber, "F.B.I. Tells of Finding Rights Victims," *The New York Times,* October 11, 1967, p. 35.

10. Ibid.

11. Walter Rugaber, "Informer Links Klan to Rights Slayings," *The New York Times,* October 12, 1967, p. 1.

12. Ibid., p. 48.

13. Linder.

14. Walter Rugaber, "Witness Tells of Role in Slaying of Rights Workers," *The New York Times,* October 13, 1967, p. 1.

15. Ibid.

16. Ibid.

17. Cagin and Dray, p. 447.

18. Rugaber, "Witness Tells of Role in Slaying of Rights Workers," p. 1.

19. Walter Rugaber, "Confession Gives Details of Three Rights Killings," *The New York Times,* October 14, 1967, p. 1.

20. Walter Rugaber, "Mississippi Jury Hears Plot Alibis," *The New York Times,* October 15, 1967, p. 64.

21. Walter Rugaber, "Trial of 18 Charged With Conspiracy in Mississippi Goes to All-White Jury," *The New York Times,* October 19, 1967, p. 37.

22. Ibid.

23. Ibid.

24. Walter Rugaber, "Deadlocked Jury Is Ordered to Continue Deliberations in Mississippi Slayings of 3 Rights Workers," *The New York Times,* October 20, 1967, p. 31.

25. *United States* v. *Allen,* 164 U.S. 492.

26. Walter Rugaber, "Mississippi Jury Convicts 7 of 18 in Rights Killings," *The New York Times,* October 21, 1967, p. 1.

27. Ibid.

Chapter 6. In the Wake of "Mississippi Burning"

1. Rhoda L. Blumberg, *Civil Rights: The 1960s Freedom Struggle* (Boston: Twayne Publishing Co., 1991), p. 126.

2. Richard Kluger, Simple Justice: *The History of* Brown *v.* Board of Education *and Black America's Struggle for Equality* (New York: Random House, 1977), p. 759.

3. Milton Viorst, *Fire in the Streets: America in the 1960s* (New York: Simon & Schuster, 1979), p. 263.

4. Kwame Ture [Stokely Carmichael] and Charles V. Hamilton, *Black Power: The Politics of Liberation in America* (New York: Random House, 1992), p. 44.

5. Harvard Sitkoff, *The Struggle for Black Equality, 1954–1992* (New York: Hill and Wang, 1993), p. 194.

6. Seth Cagin and Philip Dray, *We Are Not Afraid: The Story of Goodman, Schwerner and Chaney and the Civil Rights Campaign for Mississippi* (New York: Macmillan, 1988), pp. 455–456.

7. Joseph Lelyveld, "In America: Turning Point," *The New York Times Magazine,* April 10, 1977, p. 94.

8. Ibid.

9. Douglas O. Linder, "Bending Toward Justice: John Doar and the Mississippi Burning Trial," *Famous American Trials Page,* 2000, <http://www.law.umkc.edu/faculty/projects/ftrials/trialheroes/doaressay.html> (August 9, 2001).

9. Douglas O. Linder, "Bending Toward Justice: John Doar and the Mississippi Burning Trial," *Famous American Trials Page,* 2000, <http://www.law.umkc.edu/faculty/projects/ftrials/trialheroes/doaressay.html> (August 9, 2001).

10. Ibid.

11. Ibid.

12. Mark Ballard, "A New Look at the 'Mississippi Burning' Murders?" *National Law Journal,* September 7, 1998, p. A06.

13. Shaila Dewan, "Ex-Klansman Guilty of Manslaughter in 1964 Deaths: Revisiting Crime That Spurred Movement," *The New York Times*, June 22, 2005, pp. A1, A16; Ariel Hart, "41 Years Later, Ex-Klansman Gets 60 Years in Civil Rights Deaths," *The New York Times*, June 24, 2005, p. A14.

14. Jerry Mitchell, "Bowers: Klansman Got Away With Murder," *The Clarion-Ledger,* December 27, 1998, <http://www.clarionledger.com/crimes/burn12-27-98.html> (March 27, 2006).

15. Hart.

16. Robert S. McElvaine, "For an Old Flag, A New Rationale," *The New York Times,* April 21, 2001, p. A15.

17. Ibid.

Chronology

1. Some entries are adapted from Douglas O. Linder, "Mississippi Burning Trial: A Chronology," *Famous American Trials Page, 2000,* <http://www.law.umkc.edu/faculty/projects/ftrials/price&bowers/miss_chrono.html> (August 9, 2001).

Glossary

Congress of Racial Equality (CORE)—A civil rights group founded in 1942 to bring about social change through nonviolent means.

conspiracy—An agreement by words or actions by two or more people to accomplish an illegal act.

due process of law—A phrase in the Fifth and Fourteenth amendments to stop the federal and state governments from depriving any U.S. citizen of life, liberty, and property.

dynamite charge—A judge's instructions to a deadlocked jury to take extra time in an effort to reach a verdict.

felony—A serious crime that is subject to severe punishment under the law.

Fifteenth Amendment—Amendment added to the Constitution in 1870 to protect the rights of citizens to vote, regardless of race, color, or previous slave status.

Fourteenth Amendment—Amendment adopted in 1868 to grant the "privileges and immunities" of citizenship to former slaves. It also protected other rights of former slaves.

grand jury—A group of usually twenty-three people that decides whether there is enough evidence to bring formal charges against a suspect in a criminal case.

Ku Klux Klan—A terrorist organization formed after the Civil War to prevent former slaves from exercising their rights under the Constitution and federal law. It revived after World War I as an anti-Catholic, anti-Jewish, and anti-African American group that uses lynchings, arson, and assault to intimidate its victims.

lynching—Illegal execution. It is a tactic used primarily by the KKK.

"Mississippi Burning"—The FBI file name for a series of arson incidents, assaults, and murders against African Americans and civil rights workers in 1964.

Mississippi Freedom Democratic Party (MFDP)—A political group organized by civil rights workers in 1964 to challenge the white Democrats in the state who refused to accept racial integration and African-American voters.

nonviolence—A strategy used by Mahatma Gandhi and Martin Luther King, Jr., to protest injustice. Sit-ins and demonstrations without physical contact were common nonviolent methods used in the 1960s.

police powers—The right of states under the Tenth Amendment to regulate the health, safety, morals, and public welfare of their citizens.

poll tax—A payment required by Southern states before citizens were allowed to vote. This practice was stopped by the Twenty-Fourth Amendment, adopted in 1964.

Reconstruction—The period following the Civil War when President Lincoln and President Johnson tried to bring back into the Union those states that had seceded. It also refers to economic and political measures taken to rebuild these states while protecting the rights of former slaves.

Southern Christian Leadership Conference (SCLC)—A group led by Martin Luther King, Jr. It grew out of the yearlong effort to integrate city buses in Montgomery, Alabama, starting on December 1, 1955.

Southern Manifesto—A declaration issued by more than one hundred southern senators and congressmen that pledged to resist court-ordered integration of public schools in 1954.

Student Nonviolent Coordinating Committee (SNCC)— A civil rights group founded in 1960 that sponsored the Mississippi Freedom Summer Project.

white primaries—A method used by the Democratic party in southern states to exclude African Americans from selecting candidates who were assured of election in the so-called "Solid South," prior to the 1950s.

Further Reading

Books

Fireside, Harvey. *Plessy v. Ferguson: Separate But Equal?* Springfield, N.J.: Enslow Publishers, Inc., 1997.

Meltzer, Milton. *There Comes a Time: The Struggle for Civil Rights.* New York: Random House, 2001.

Rochelle, Belinda. *Young People Who Fought for Civil Rights.* Madison, Wisc.: Turtleback Books, 1997.

Sitkoff, Harvard. *The Struggle for Black Equality, 1954–1992.* New York: Hill & Wang, 1993.

Walton, Anthony. *Mississippi: An American Journey.* New York: Alfred Knopf, 1996.

Internet Addresses

Famous American Trials

"U.S. vs Cecil Price et al. ('Mississippi Burning' Trial)"
<http://www.law.umkc.edu/faculty/projects/ftrials/price&bowers/price&bowers.htm>

Jurist—The Legal Education Network

Famous Trials: The Mississippi Burning Trial
<http://jurist.law.pitt.edu/trials8.htm>

Index